The 12-Minute M
Book 3

How to Create the Conditions For Great Work

Practical inspiration to help you create habits, relationships and mindsets that will enable your genius to emerge

Robbie Swale

Winds of Trust Publications

Contents

Part Two: CREATE THE PEOPLE AND RELATIONSHIPS YOU NEED

Part Three: CREATE ATTITUDES, MINDSETS AND MENTAL MODELS TO HELP YOU THRIVE

We can't control creativity – it's too complex for that – but we can make ourselves creativity-prone. We can create the conditions that enable our greatest work to emerge.

Impact

'Many times, in many ways, I have recommended the 12-Minute Method to others and watched them come alive with inspiration when they hear how Robbie brought this book to life. His genius ideas are exponentially valuable. To me, it's the 12-Minute Miracle.'

Michelle C. Basey

Energy Healing Artist and CoreYou Coach

'As a true believer in the power of creativity to fire us up and get us into action, I see Robbie as a real leader in the field. His ability to excite and inspire even the most reluctant participants is really impressive. Whether in academia, tech, finance, culture or anything in between, Robbie will help you put aside the noise and focus on what is really important to you.'

Jo Hunter

Co-Founder and CEO, 64 Million Artists

'Robbie's writing and 12-Minute Method inspired me to finally take the first steps to start a business I'd had in my mind (and done nothing about) for years. Learning to lean into resistance and just take the first step has had a huge impact on my mindset, mental health, family and career development. In the four years since, we have become a successful, award-winning business! I'm extremely grateful to Robbie for his genuinely impactful and thought-provoking 12-minute articles.'

Paul Thompson

Founder/Health and Wellbeing Coach and Consultant, WorkSmart Wellbeing

'I would highly recommend Robbie to anyone who is facing what feels like an insurmountable hurdle, whether it's personal or professional.'

Emma Kerr

Senior Global Practice Specialist, DAI

'I wouldn't have written any of what I have without Robbie's example and his 12-minute approach. It's what gave me the initial courage to try such a writing practice myself, to break through both fear and creative blockage…and then to post one article, then several, then to become known for such writing. When someone mentioned I should write a book, the only thing that gave me the confidence to believe I could was seeing what Robbie had already accomplished. I am on page 316 of my flash draft.'

Peter Tavernise

Leadership Coach

'The ethos of the 12-Minute Method is inspiring and challenging, but it is hearing what led Robbie to it in the first place that connects most. Words matter, but so does the spirit and story behind the words, and that's what catches me more than anything about Robbie's writing.'

Dr Hannah Mather

Executive Coach, Theologian, and Author, The Interpreting Spirit

'Robbie will get an acknowledgment in my second book, as he did in my first. The second couldn't have been written without the first and my first would never have been written without Robbie's leadership and his 12-Minute Method. His fingerprints are for evermore on anything I publish! Robbie's guidance will support your progress and will lead you to share the 12-Minute Method with others. It's that good.'

David W. Reynolds

Creator and Host of the Lead. Learn. Change. Podcast; Author, Lead. Learn. Change

'I was paralysed by fear and indecision until I came across Robbie's work. Now, thanks to the 12-Minute Method, I believe that I am an author and I am writing my first book.'

Nadine Kelly, M.D.,

Founder of NPK Health Integration

'"Surely I can find 12 minutes in a day," I thought when I saw Robbie's workshop on how to write a book in 12 minutes. It was a low barrier to entry towards creating a sustainable writing practice. It was the best decision I have made. I have now published a book and have been writing for 483 consecutive days. I would not have done that had it not been for Robbie's idea, but more importantly seeing him walk his talk with the 12-Minute Method.'

Karena de Souza

Author, Contours of Courageous Parenting

'I've always liked to write. However, I'm not a writer. Why would I write, if I'm not a writer? Stumbling upon Robbie's 12-Minute Method gave me permission to write. Anyone can be a writer for 12 minutes! Since incorporating the method into my weekly routine, and publishing on social, I am considered by many to be a "thought leader" in my space.'

Bryon Howard

CEO, The Howard Team Real Estate Services – eXp Realty

'Each time I talk with Robbie, he gives me a new thought to think about.'

Robert Holden

Author, Authentic Success

'Whatever progress you wish you could make in your career, or more generally in your life – whether it's starting a business, writing your first book, or any other new beginning – Robbie's 12-Minute Method will help you overcome the obstacles in your way, focus your energy and start!'

Alex Swallow
Author, How To Become An Influencer

About the Author

Written on 13th October, 2021

I'm Robbie Swale, a writer and coach.

There have been many times in my life where I didn't get my ideas off the ground, where I was stuck in creative hell and where I wasn't productive. Where my potential was underused. Thankfully, mostly that has changed.

Now people call me prolific and that's all down to the lessons I learned while creating the 12-Minute Method. Some of the things I have beaten procrastination to do and finally got off the ground include:

- A blog, clocking in at over 250 articles; each written in 12 minutes

- A coaching business, built from nothing, that could support me full-time in less than two years

- *Aprendiendo español* (I've got a long way to go, but I've been keeping going for more than four years now)

- A website dedicated to my favourite author, now containing over 300 inspirational snippets of wisdom (read more at **www.wisdomofgemmell.com**)

- A podcast, including interviews with best-selling authors and world-famous coaches (**www.thecoachsjourney.com**)

- Books: three out now including this one, one more due in 2022, and another that's almost finished
- A career change
- Getting married

I spent the first decade of my career doing lots of different things. I was a director, a trustee, a manager, almost a professional actor, a leader and an administrator.

In my current work, I'm interested in three things:

Creativity (and why people don't do the things they want to do). That's where this book and the 12-Minute Method Series fit in.

Leadership and how people can be honourable in their work while achieving great things. How they can find success without feeling like they have to compromise their values and identity. That, after all, is what allows them to do their best work.

Coaching: the amazing craft that allows each of us to develop vital skills for our future, to more often be our wisest and most skilful selves, and to move closer to fulfilling our potential.

I've coached people working on amazing creative ideas, from businesses to books and beyond. I've worked with people on many incredible projects that you will never have heard of. I've also worked, coached, trained and facilitated for organisations like Swiss Re, the University of Edinburgh, the Royal Opera House, Moonpig, UCL and more.

I'm proud to be an associate of 64 Million Artists, an organisation dedicated to unleashing the creativity of everyone in the UK, and a Fellow Coach for BetterUp, the world's biggest mental health and coaching organisation.

Mostly, though, I'm proud that I've spent a decade now truly committed to doing my best work. To making the most of my potential. To releasing my unique genius into the world. And in doing that I'm proud that I've felt fear, felt resistance, felt the pull of procrastination, and I've battled it, knowing that that battle was a battle for my soul: to take me out of creative hell and grow me into someone new. There have been many ideas that haven't made it because I didn't know how to fight that battle. But my line is drawn: *not anymore.*

Read more about me and sign up to my mailing list at
www.robbieswale.com

About This Book

In the previous two books in the 12-Minute Method series, I've started out by writing something like: 'This is not a 'how to' book in the traditional sense.' In fact, I wrote that just now, and then I realised that…well, this is more of a 'how to' book, in the traditional sense, than books one and two.

Not that it is 'six easy steps to do more great work' or anything like that. And it certainly doesn't 'guarantee' great work.

As I wrote in the opening pages, creativity is complex. Doing great work is complex. And anyone who tries to pretend that there is a simple route to those things is – in my opinion – wrong.

But this book contains many ways that you could change your life to do more great work, to fulfil your potential more, to enable your genius to emerge.

There are other people who have – with integrity – tried to map the process of enabling genius to emerge, but that's not how I create. My creations, including this book, are a drawing together of many influences and a synthesising of those influences and ideas into one place.

Here, in this book, you'll find over 40 chapters, and the truth is that each – although I didn't know this as I wrote them – can be a meditation to create an insight that helps you to do more great work.

So use this book in whatever way makes sense to you.

It has been arranged to be read cover-to-cover, start to finish, with an arc that makes sense. You could do that. It will be a relatively quick read, with short, accessible chapters. But even more than the other books in the series, it might benefit from being read slowly. Less, in this book, is there a single message. More there is a wealth of textured ideas, any of which might be the practical inspiration you need.

This means the order doesn't matter *so* much. You could just dip in at random, and trust that the universe will present you with the idea that is most relevant and useful to you today. Creativity is so complex that this might actually be a better way to read the book than cover to cover.

Or of course you could scan the contents and look for the chapter title that feels like it will speak to you today.

Whatever way you read it, I want to invite you to read for insight.

As I was preparing this book for publication I realised that, more than the other books in the series, this one really does have the potential, on any page, to provide you with the insight you need. Many of the pieces could appear in more than one part of the book, because they contain ideas about action *and* mindset, relationships *and* habits, attitudes *and* ideas. Reading them back, even I was struck by ideas I had almost forgotten and their potential power.

So set the intention to read for insight that might change your ways of working, your mindset, your relationships *forever*. And when you notice the feeling of an insight, that sense of possibility, make sure you make a note.

If you want help with that, I've created a worksheet to record your insights as you go. For some of us it's very easy to 'just' read a book and not put the ideas in it into action. If that's you, you might want to download that worksheet here:

www.robbieswale.com/12minute-method-downloads

Most importantly, make use of what's in this book. It's collected from many people in many disciplines (I've noted some of the most-cited people on the worksheet above) and it contains many of the ideas that have helped me to believe that I am doing more great work now than I was last year, and more last year than the year before that.

Later in the book, you'll find the powerful idea of comparing yourself to you yesterday, not to someone else today. Do that as you read this book. Remember that you are on *your* journey to doing great work, to fulfilling your potential, to enabling your unique genius.

That is important. And so, make sure that you use this book in whatever way will help you do that.

That's what it was designed for. Well, kind of. More on that next.

Robbie Swale
12th July, 2022

The 12-Minute Method

Written on 12th July, 2022

About 10 years ago – almost to the day, in fact – my long-term relationship ended. It often seems that when a relationship like that ends a huge amount of energy is released into the lives of the people whose relationship has ended. Not always positive energy, of course, but as I heard the author Katharine Woodward-Thomas say years later, to make the best of break-ups and divorces, harnessing that energy for the best can be very powerful. If you can manage it, all kinds of change can happen.

I didn't know at the time, but thanks to the support I had around me and who knows what else, I harnessed that energy of change. Over the next two years I moved jobs and then left that one, realising that I needed to leave behind the career as a leader in the arts that I had been developing. I travelled the world, fulfilling what I hadn't realised was a gap in my needs for travel, growing as a human and creating a separation in which to look at my life.

And I picked up a thread I had previously looked at closely: how do I do my best work? How do I find a calling? How do I do *great* work?

I had first seen these questions starkly when I pursued a career in acting. Auditioning for the best drama schools in the UK, I came within what felt like inches of a place at almost all the leading institutions…and then received no offers. As I sat with that disappointment (sandwiched between two years of auditions where I didn't get close at all), I noticed two things: one was that I didn't want a career where my success or failure would rest so much on the whims of someone else. Another, more importantly, was that I reflected on what it would mean if I was an actor. And I realised if I pursued that, I would end up leaving behind so many parts of me that were not needed in that career.

Acting would leave behind some of the parts of me that had made me a student leader aged 21, part of a team running an organisation with hundreds of staff and a turnover of millions of pounds.

And it would leave behind the parts of me that admired the TV characters I was watching who were getting things done and having impact on an enormous scale.

And, in the end, acting wasn't for me.

I picked up that thread again in the aftermath of that relationship: working in the arts hadn't worked out. I loved the things we had made happen, but the actual work? I could feel that that work was not what I wanted to be doing. I was drained by it. And I kept realising that other people wouldn't be. If others would thrive off this work, then was I really using myself well?

And so, as I picked up the thread, I wondered: what work

could I do where I would love doing the *actual work*? What work would I love to read about in my spare time? And how could I find the thing in the centre of a Venn diagram I heard consultant Brett Thomas describe: the intersection of what I loved, what I was good at and the contribution I wanted to make to the world.

After several false starts, I found coaching. It fulfilled those criteria. I didn't know for sure that it would, but it felt good – as I wrote in *How to Start When You're Stuck*, I ran my career change (and then my business) on a one-line business plan: follow the feeling. And I had the feeling with coaching.

It was all those things. And, it was hard.

As part of my commitment to fulfilling my potential, to using *all* my gifts, to hitting the middle of Thomas' Venn diagram, I hired a coach. I knew that was important.

Then, in August 2016, I was on a call with my coach, Joel Monk. We had been working on the idea of sharing myself with the world. It filled me with anxiety.

It hadn't always been like that. As an actor I promoted my plays. In my work in the arts I wrote for the local paper. I created things and, in some cases, had the courage to share them.

But at that moment, even posting a joke on Facebook caused me anxiety. It would get written, thought about for a disproportionately long time and then deleted.

Even that caused me anxiety. Let alone the idea of *really* sharing myself.

But I'd been reading *The War of Art* by Steven Pressfield. It's about winning our creative battles and beating Resistance, Pressfield's concept of a universal force that holds us back from changing things in our lives and the world. This idea has been so important to me that you'll find references to it throughout this book. One of the things he says is something like this: the rule of thumb for Resistance is that the more Resistance you feel towards something, the more important it is for your soul's evolution.

I *knew* that sharing myself with the world was important. Not just logistically, although it's hard to run a coaching business without some online presence. On an intuitive level at least, I knew that sharing myself was important for my soul's evolution; for my opportunity to evolve and grow into my potential, into what was really possible for me.

And, looking back, I can't help but be amazed at how true that was.

Joel and I were discussing creating something that I could share. I liked the freedom of my short train journey from Clapham Junction in south west London to London Waterloo. It felt like there I was free from the pressure of doing more, being more, and 'getting on with things'.

Perhaps the key moment, and one full of meaning for my life, came when Joel shared that in his previous work as a visual artist he liked to create series of paintings. What if I created a series?

And so, the Train Series was born. It was designed to help me to practice sharing things; *sharing* them, not making things that are perfect. I would write an article on the train like this: I would write while the train was moving, stop when the train stopped, proofread what I had written once and then post it online. I thought I'd post it on LinkedIn because…well, I thought no one read LinkedIn.

I decided I would create a series of five articles over the next two weeks: one on each day I travelled into London.

And then it turned out some people *did* read LinkedIn. Mostly, these days, I would advise people to create for themselves and let the audience come, but in that moment the fact that some people 'Liked' the articles I'd written really meant something.

Not many 'Likes' – and not all of the articles got any – but some. The occasional comment.

And most importantly for all my fears: no one laughed at me, no one said they were terrible, no one hated me. Those were the fears, hiding not far beneath the surface.

After those two weeks and five articles I went away on holiday. I said I was going to think about what would happen next, but I already knew that *something* would happen next. I had the feeling.

It wasn't that the articles and sharing them was *fun* or *nice*, but it was *good*. It was the right thing for me to do.

I made it a weekly practice until Christmas. And then I continued it. I have been writing an article a week in that way for almost six years as I write this. There are more than 250 of them (I don't write on holidays, and I have missed a few weeks here and there for all kinds of reasons).

After a while, I stopped going into the city as much and I wanted a way to write when there wasn't a train journey. I checked how long the journey took the next time I was on the train, and it took about 12 minutes. And so, from then on, when I wasn't getting the train I would write with a 12-minute timer: write while the timer is going, stop when it stops, proofread it once and post it online.

And there, in one way, is the 12-Minute Method.

But that's not everything.

Because something else was happening. Something strange.

About three years into the 12-minute blog, inspired a little by marketing guru Seth Godin, I realised I could turn the posts I'd written so far into a book. LinkedIn is hard to navigate and if anyone wanted to read all of my blog it would actually be really hard. For 10 people who I imagined might want to do that, and for the 10 I thought I might meet in the next three years who might want to do the same, having a book of the blog would be really useful.

And I should say that one of the ways I beat my Resistance to sharing is to remind myself that if it helps even one person, it's worth me facing my fears and insecurities.

I also thought it would be funny. I could call it *I Wrote This Book in 12 Minutes*.

I enlisted the help of my friend Steve Creek to edit this book. And as we discussed it in Doppio Coffee on Battersea Park Road, he asked me a great question. It was something like this: 'That title is great. It's an inspiration to people to do their thing, to get on with it. Can the book do that, too?'

Can the book help people do the things they're struggling to do?

And it turned out, truly miraculously as I think back, that it could.

I sat down and thought about the stages of the creative process; the stages that we all need help with if we want to make something that matters. I printed off three years of blog posts and I started dealing them out.

It turned out that they fell, almost perfectly, into those stages.

A few didn't, and there were a few overlaps, too – those can be found in the eBook *The Cutting Room* at:

www.robbieswale.com/12minute-method-downloads

But the rest of them did. I couldn't believe it. I hadn't just written 80,000 words (although that's what 12 minutes a week for three years will get you); I had written 80,000 words about how to do the things that we really want to do.

Of course, this shouldn't have surprised me.

I had been writing from intuition every week. In 12 minutes there's not much time to think, and I was almost always writing about what I was most interested in that week – what felt most important. And throughout those three years I'd been leaning into my resistance, procrastination and fear in order to run my business, to write my articles, and to be present and vulnerable in the world.

Not only that, but my business was coaching. In some ways, describing coaching is really simple: it's helping people do the thing they want to do that for some reason they aren't doing. So not only had I been wrestling with my Resistance, but I'd been helping other people with theirs, too.

And so here I had it. A book about that. With four clear stages. Later, I decided the book would be more accessible as a series of four short books than as one long book, and so those four stages are the four books in the 12-Minute Method series.

So the 12-Minute Method is, absolutely, to sit for 12 minutes a week to work on what matters. And the great thing about '12 minutes' is that it's completely arbitrary: the train mostly doesn't even take that long. Your 12-minute method might in fact involve 19 or 3 or 46 minutes each week.

But the 12-Minute Method is more than that. It is this four-stage process that I identified over years of struggle and supporting people with their struggles. To make work that matters, here's what you have to do:

You have to start. That's the most important thing. Everything that matters was at one point started and nothing you want to create will exist unless *you* start it. That's what *How to Start When You're Stuck* is about.

You have to keep going. If you give up, if you quit, you won't see the full possibility of what you could create. You have to start again, every day. That's what *How to Keep Going When You Want to Give Up* is about. And as I reflected on this stage for the book, I realised that something else happens if you can stick with a habit over weeks or months: you start to see that over a long period of time everything is possible. If I can write a book in 12 minutes each week, and I now know (because I have these books as evidence) that I'm someone who can stick with their habit over years, then what else can I do? Well, almost anything.

And then, if you want to do as much great work as you can, there are things you can do to help that happen. You have to create the conditions for your best work to emerge. That's what this book is about.

Finally, if you want your work to make as big a difference as it can, you have to share it. You have to make it possible for it to change that *one* other person. Who might of course turn out to be ten, or a hundred, or a thousand, or millions. You have to share your work.

And so the 12-Minute Method is this four-stage process:

1. Start.
2. Keep going.
3. Create the conditions for great work.
4. Share it.

The order matters. And it's especially important for me to say that in this book. Many creative projects, including mine, have been wrecked on the rocks of 'getting things just right'. So I want to say this clearly:

If you want to do great work, the **NUMBER ONE CONDITION FOR CREATING GREAT WORK** is to **START**.

This is also important:

If you want to do great work, the **NUMBER TWO CONDITION FOR CREATING GREAT WORK** is to **KEEP GOING**.

Only after that should you think about what is in this book.

To demonstrate why this is important, it's worth talking about Chapter One of this book. It remains probably the best 12-minute article I have written. It reached thousands of people in a matter of days, including the author who inspired it, Fred Kofman. It is listed as recommended reading on a training programme he runs. It is great work. It brought me to tears as I read it back recently when bringing this book together. And it came after years of practice.

If I hadn't started, it wouldn't exist. And if I hadn't kept going for more than two years, it wouldn't exist.

So if you want to do great work, find your practice (whether it takes 12-minutes a week or something different), start practising and keep practising.

But despite that, the contents of this book are vitally important.

Emerging into my work over the seven years since I started coaching has been an ever-growing sense of the importance of supporting the people I come into contact with to do great work, whatever that means for them.

It is almost impossible to know how to change the world. The world, like creativity, is so complex. So many things we do make some things worse even while making others better. I've thought about this a lot, and listened to a lot of other people talking about this, too. Here's where I've come to on how we can all help:

We can think, carefully, about how to do our absolute best work. How to combine our talents and interests into fulfilling our potential.

Then we can do everything we can to be our wisest, most noble selves. That way we can be as sure as we can that we are making things better and not worse.

That is what the 12-Minute Method series is about. It's about unleashing the untapped potential of those of us stuck in creative hell, knowing what we want to do, knowing how it will change us and the world around us but not doing it. Helping people step towards fulfilling their potential. Helping you step out of creative hell and into what is possible for you. Helping you do great work.

There are so many ways to do that, but in this book I have separated the ideas I collected over those three years into three sections.

There are things we can *do* to create the conditions for great work. Actions we can take, habits we can create. These are practical things that will get us out of our own way and allow our genius to emerge. They are test-driven by me and by people I have spoken to. You can hear that in the writing. You'll find the actions and habits in Part One of this book.

There are *relationships* we need to create. No one in the 21st century will do their best work completely alone. And even those who look like they do will know, deep inside, that the people who love and support them are as much a part of their work as they are. That's what the dedications and acknowledgements in every book you've ever read tell us. Part Two of this book is about creating the relationships we need to create great work.

There are things we can *think*, ways we can *be*, that create the conditions for great work. That's what Part Three is about. It's about mindsets, attitudes and ideas that will help you do your best work, that will enable the unique genius inside you to emerge.

Because I do believe that there's a genius inside you. One of the biggest insights of the last seven years for me has been just how much I believe practise matters, and how little talent really counts. That means that genius, really, is just a combination of two things: understand who you really are, and then practise using that as much as you can until the genius inside you emerges.

Other people, like Gay Hendricks and Myles Downey and Matthew Syed, have written more about that in their own ways – ways that have inspired me. And you can go and read their books to find out more.

But first, read this one. In here are ideas from people like them, distilled to provide you with the practical inspiration you need to release your genius, to fulfil your potential, and to do great work.

Don't forget what I said: the most important conditions for great work are to start working and to keep going.

But after that, maybe the next most important condition for you will be found in this book.

We can't be sure of much when it comes to something as complex as creativity. The philosopher Ken Wilber once said something like this: enlightenment is a bit like having an accident. You can't *make* yourself enlightened, but you can make yourself enlightenment-prone.

Well, creativity is like that, too. And doing great work. Too complex to control, but possible to enable.

Keep your eyes peeled for that little something that might make you more prone to doing great work.

That might enable your genius just a little bit more.

I hope you find it.

I want to see your great work.

I want it to change the world.

Free 12-Minute Method Action Sheet

I want you to use this book to help you create the conditions that enable you to do great work. And so I've created a worksheet that guides you through creating your own 12-minute practice and gives you somewhere to turn the insights you get from this book into action.

It also includes some recommended further reading from the thinkers and authors who have influenced this book and the rest of the series, whose names you'll find in the chapters that follow.

You can download the action sheet for free at:

www.robbieswale.com/12minute-method-downloads
or by scanning this QR code:

Remember: the most important condition for great work is that you start working.

Don't forget: the second-most important condition for great work is that you don't give up.

Part One: CREATE ACTIONS, HABITS AND PATTERNS THAT ENABLE YOUR BEST WORK

If we want to do great work, there are actions that we have to take to help us get there. That's what Part One is about. It's about the things you might do.

Some of these pieces are pure and simple: structures or practices that I or my clients have used. Or key areas, like rest or solitude, that almost everyone who wants to do great work will spend at least some time thinking about.

But many are more complex: Chapter One contains several exercises you can do, but it is also about one of most fundamental mindset shifts that will get you into action, and into doing great work and not holding back.

Other chapters are about ways to think about your action, ways to change your habits and more.

In some of the chapters, you can hear me wrestling with the challenges of this: the balances that need to be inquired into and found. I can't tell you how to create your perfect balances – if balance is even the correct word – but these inquiries, too, are vital. To have thought about them, have made your best guess for now, and have put that into action, is far more likely to create the conditions for your best work than to leave these important thoughts unconscious.

There are many, many ways that you might create the conditions for great work in practical ways, through patterns, habits, actions and more.

Look for the insights that support you and – if you find them, if you get that feeling – *take action.*

Chapter One
It's Time for You to Die

Written on 5th October, 2018

It's time for you to die. Right now. Take a chance – in *this* moment – that I am right, and your world can change forever.

I don't mean literally die, of course. Although, for countless people across the world, in this second it *is* their time. And one day, it will be yours. That, truly and deeply, is the only certainty of life. You will live and you will die.

So take a chance, now, to die before you die. To free yourself from the ties that bind you – the fears that hold you back, mostly falsely in the modern world – and free yourself from fear of death. It is a deep fear and a human fear. Facing death, in those moments where we have to, is terrifying. I'm lucky enough never to have literally faced my own death but I have witnessed others facing their death. And I have felt the waves of tragedy or potential tragedy near me.

And this fear of death, it stops you living. As the character of William Wallace says in the movie *Braveheart*: 'Every man dies. Not every man really lives.'

Come with me now, to a place where you may not be comfortable, to die before you die. And in doing that, to be freed to live the life deep within you. The kind of life you admire in others, the kind of life that your Higher Self is being called to live.

David Treleaven speaks of working with clients to make them a commitment to this life, the life deep within them. He asks them the questions. Something like: 'At your end of your life, what would make you sad? What things that you would have done, or not done?' He then guides them to living as a commitment to the alternatives to these things, to the things that matter deeply to them. The kind of things that perhaps only in facing death will you to be brave enough to regret.

Fred Kofman asks questions in his workshops: imagine that you have only three minutes to live, and you want to make one final phone call to someone. Whom would you call? What would you tell that person?

He then says: 'And what are you waiting for?'

When you only have three minutes to live – and at some point in your life, you *will* only have three minutes to live, even if you don't know it in that moment – you may not be able to do that thing, or to call that person. So call them now. He says that in the break following this part of his workshops he sees people on the phone, having deeply meaningful conversations. Conversations that may change them and the people they are speaking with forever.

Fred also talks about bringing people, deeply, into dying

before they die. He explains the exercise in his brilliant book, *The Meaning Revolution: The Power of Transcendent Leadership*. First, imagine you have lived a long and rich life, and when you find out you are going to die your friends hold a living funeral for and with you. In the ceremony, a dear friend will speak a eulogy.

Write the eulogy you would want your friend to give. Don't be humble, be true.

Fred then takes them to a darker place: a place where we may not be as comfortable to go. Imagine you have just died, with no chance to make any changes in your life. Then answer these questions, in the third person as the devil's advocate or regretful friend, speaking after your death:

What dreams did X not pursue? What fears did X not overcome? What loves did X not express? What resentments did X not resolve? What apologies did X not make? What gifts did X not give?

These are the questions for you to answer today, if you want your life to change.

These, and: what, if you came to the end of your life, would make you sad? What, then are you a commitment to?

These, and: if you only had three minutes to live – right now – what would you do, who would you call? Then do it. Then call them.

Today, again following Fred's leadership, I entered a coaching call with the intention: *serve my client like it's the last day of my life and the last conversation I'll ever have.* My normal intention is 'serve powerfully', and it leads me to doing great work. But this conversation was different. It was deeper. I didn't hold back, I didn't make nice or be polite for its own sake, just when it was natural. I caught myself when I hesitated and I spoke from a deeper, more truthful place in me. It has reinvigorated my work with this client.

So ask yourself the questions. They may be uncomfortable. They may be full of fear. They should be. I am asking you to face death. But you can do it. Because you are brave.

Come die with me, today.

Then come live with me, tomorrow.

Chapter Two

The Power of a Vision in a Complex World

Written on 28th March, 2019

People tell the story of John F. Kennedy and the race to put a man on the moon something like this: he put his vision out into the world. *We are going to put a man on the moon.* He didn't know what was going to happen, he didn't know how they were going to do it, but he put the vision out there and so it happened.

But there's another space race story that I like better. It stars Kennedy again. This time he went to visit the NASA headquarters. He met a janitor there, and asked: 'What do you do here?'

The janitor said: 'I'm helping put a man on the moon.'

That's the power of a vision: it invites people to be part of it.

I was talking to a client today about the difference between this – stating a vision at the visionary level, which invites people to see themselves as a part of that vision, a contributor to something important – and giving a vision with all the details already filled in. In the latter case you might say, this is what we're working towards, this is what we are going to do, this is what we need in order to do it.

It might seem like the latter is a better vision, or a better business plan, but I don't think so, and especially not in the complex world we live in.

In a world that gives leaders problems as wicked and complex as the race to put a man on the moon on a regular basis, it is tempting to think that a more detailed plan of action will help us get there. But, as Jennifer Garvey Berger says in her latest book, *Unlocking Leadership Mindtraps: How to Thrive in Complexity*, in a complex world, much as we hope for control, most of the time the control we think we create is a myth anyway. Or it traps us into controlling pointless things just because they are measurable, not because they help us achieve what we want to achieve. Instead of trying to control things, better by far to *create conditions for things to thrive.*

That's what Kennedy was doing as he offered that vision. He was saying: here is a vision, a vision to capture the human soul. How are we going to get there? I don't know. That's why I have all you scientists – and janitors – who can make it happen.

Kennedy's job was to create the conditions for magic to happen. That's what I aim to do with my clients and it's what you could aim to do, too, in whatever way you lead in the world. Don't try to control things, as it's only a mirage anyway and mostly it gets in the way of what you want to achieve. Instead, create conditions for magic to happen –

including a vision that captures the human soul – and even you may be surprised by what you can achieve.

Chapter Three
How to Change Your Habits

Written on 26ᵗʰ August, 2016

Habits are hard to change.

I kept pulling muscles in my back. Not badly, but every few months. I wasn't sure what was causing it, but I set out to try to change some habits that I thought might help. My warm-up, with a back stretch every morning, was relatively easy to change. My posture, when sitting and running, much harder. It started with putting my attention on my posture. Notice, when I can. Change, when I notice. Don't blame when I don't.

That last part is important for lasting change.

I'm trying to change another health-related habit now. I carry a lot of tension in my jaw, which has some downsides for my teeth, and sometimes for opening my mouth. I'm using the same technique to change how I hold my mouth when I walk and sit, when I lean my chin on my hand, and several other things. After my other experiences, I am confident the habits will change.

Notice, when I can. Change, when I notice. Don't blame when I don't.

It's relatively easy to notice when I need to change a physical habit. My body tells me (or my dentist does).

What about mental habits? What about emotional habits? What about habits that are ingrained even longer, from childhood? What about those stories we have been telling ourselves, about ourselves, about others, about the world? For years. Maybe decades.

Well, I don't know for sure. Everyone's habits are different, just as everyone's stories are different. But I'm pretty sure it starts with noticing, when you can. Followed by changing, when you notice, if you can. And in those cases it is even more important not to blame, when you don't.

And of course, you have to want the habit, the story, to change.

Chapter Four

A Single Question That Can Change Your Life

Written on 21ˢᵗ December, 2017

I'm part of a group programme for coaches at the moment, run by Rich Litvin, co-author of the influential book for coaches, *The Prosperous Coach*.

One of the powerful parts of this programme is a weekly report submitted by each member. It contains a number of questions and trackers to help the members of the programme on their coaching and leadership journeys.

The question that has probably had the biggest effect on me so far is this:

Which one thing that drains me of energy will I stop doing this week?

Now I should know this – this is the kind of thing I say to clients regularly – but putting your attention on something has a remarkable effect. In this case, it brings that week's drain on your energy into consciousness every time it happens or you find yourself doing it. And then, instead of following your usual downward spiral of reactions, you are able to make a choice: '*Here I am doing this thing again. Was I just paying lip service in my weekly report or did I really mean it? Am I going to allow this thing to drain my energy now or am I going to find a different way to deal with it?'*

Here are some of the answers I have given so far: avoiding opening emails from prospective clients about whether they want to work with me out of fear of 'No'; getting dragged into areas of capability and urgency at the expense of the magic and most important; worrying.

This week my answer is: worrying about money but doing nothing to raise my awareness or consciousness of my actual financial position.

And here's what's happened. Already, hours after writing it, I've put in place a further plan to, in the long term, take action on this more and more. It just came to me as I walked to the train. How useful.

And, at this time of year, when we're all thinking about how we might work on ourselves over the next year, to change our life for the better, to make ourselves and our loved ones even happier, I want to offer this frame to you: which one thing that drains me of energy will I stop doing this week?

I like it because it doesn't hold the overwhelm of a resolution like 'learn to swim' or 'get a new job' or even 'be happier'; and because I don't need to (fail to) remember it over a long period, which can happen even when taking a 'theme' for the year. These may work for you, but they don't really for me.

And I like it because it feeds the theme of the journey I've been on, of continuing to choose a better path for myself and others, each and every day.

It's gentle, and it's effective. Each week, make a choice and a commitment. You may not have a group that you've paid a lot of money to be part of (that's what it took for me to get into this practice), but anyone can use the apps Randomly Remind Me or Mind Jogger, or set a weekly reminder in their Google calendar.

My commitment for the next year is that every week, even after the work with Rich is over, I will ask myself: 'Which one thing that drains me of energy will I stop doing this week?'

Join me?

Chapter Five

How I Work Through Sadness and Fragility Each Morning

Written on 3rd July, 2019

I often feel sad and fragile in the morning. Not every morning, not all the time. But most mornings.

I try not to check my phone, because if I do and there's a message there that says the wrong thing, or a tweet about the wrong issue, then I'll find myself locked in an anxious contraction. I turned off email alerts on my phone partly for this reason, to give myself a chance in the morning.

It's not because my life isn't good, by the way. By any measure I can think of, it's better than it has ever been. But I don't jump out of bed in delight, skipping across the bedroom with cartoon birds singing round my head. I lie there, wishing I didn't have to get up, feeling sad or anxious about the day ahead.

Psychologist Jonathan Haidt talks about this example – knowing it is sensible to get up, but still not moving – as proof that our rational brain isn't as in control as we think it is: if our instincts want to stay in bed then we stay in bed.

For me, it's just a part of the pattern of life. When I spoke to a friend of mine last year, she thought being miserable in the mornings was proof that she needed to change her job. Now, it may well have been the right thing for her to change her job, but for me there is no correlation (let alone causation) between feeling miserable in the morning and doing powerful work that fulfils me and changes the world for the better.

I often feel miserable in the morning. Here's what I do to help with that.

In the end, I get up (after wrestling with my instincts for a while, and often ill-advisedly checking my phone and getting dragged by my instincts yet again into some dopamine-friendly app).

I put my exercise gear on and I go to the gym. I know from the consultant and author Eve Poole that there is research that shows that the only way to break down stress hormones is exercise and also that you can fuel yourself up ahead of time. So I go to the gym and I do some lifting and some cardio. It's not a particularly well-planned or efficient workout, but it's good enough. It gets my heart pumping, gets the endorphins flowing. While I'm at the gym, I listen to something, a podcast. Nothing too stressful, as I'm still trying to protect myself in a fragile morning state. Nothing political, usually, and certainly no news. Often a football podcast, sometimes Tim Ferriss, sometimes a different interview, sometimes a documentary. Occasionally something political, actually, if I'm feeling secure enough.

I come home and eat my breakfast. It's not a perfect

breakfast (too many carbs, maybe) but it's not terrible (sugar only via banana, protein via almonds). While I'm eating it, I drink a lot of water (dehydration is a common reason for feeling off-centre) and take a multivitamin (I trust the placebo effect will make sure I gain something from it, even if most of the vitamins will pass through my system). I sit, as I do this, and I read. Usually fiction: I'm still easing myself in to the day, protecting myself from things that might stress me until I'm feeling secure.

Then I shower and dress and make a cup of coffee.

I sit down with the cup of coffee and as I drink it, I read again. Usually this is about 15 minutes of non-fiction, which is often my entire helping of non-fiction for the day.

At some point during this routine, towards the end, my phone will buzz with the question: 'What is in best service of your goals today?' I write the answer to this in a note on my phone, and check if I did what I said was most important the day before (marking 'did this' if I did it, or what happened if I didn't, or noting that I didn't do it yesterday if I forgot).

And then I'm ready to start work. If I have a coaching call first, I'll do two short meditations to prepare myself and warm myself up for my work. If not, I'll ease into whatever is most important.

I go to a lot of trouble to make sure that I work myself through the sadness I feel in the morning, the fragility, and build myself a solid foundation for the day.

It started bit-by-bit and evolved month-by-month and year-by-year. On different days each part of this feels like the part that makes the most difference, the part I love the most.

You might not have the freedom to do all these things, but you can do *some* of them if you choose to. You can do a little more today than you did yesterday.

For me, by accident, I now have something to answer Tim Ferriss if he ever asks me to tell him about my morning routine.

Chapter Six
Give Yourself a Break

Written on 15th June, 2017

Coming back after a holiday always makes me reassess things. I guess it's a part of being a curious person. Having a practice like this, where I have to write something and post it, only encourages me.

Often, having a break gets me thinking about how I feel after I've had one. What is the effect on me of some time off? This week, particularly on Monday and Tuesday after flying back from Crete on Sunday, I felt tired. And yet, it was such a different tired to the tired I felt before I left. This was tiredness, yes, but before I left I was drained. Not because I don't like my work (although I've had that in the past). Perhaps, in fact, because I really like it. I drive myself hard. This week, I'm tired because I've quickly gotten used to staying in bed and then sitting by the pool enjoying the sun and now I am making myself do something quite different.

I'm coming through that now, though. I'm adjusting to working again and I can feel the difference. When I spoke to my friend Nicole yesterday, she said 'I like this Robbie'. 'This Robbie' is particularly laid back and relaxed. And that, if you ask me, is the effect of a break.

I coach better after a break. I sell coaching better after a break. I am also happier and more relaxed after a break, even when under pressure, as I felt last night having an interview for a training course at 11.30pm due to time zone difference.

And here's what I think. I think *we all know this*. We all know we work better after a break. When we are looking after ourselves. When we find the right balance. But we don't *trust* it.

We can't quite believe that by taking a break we could become *more productive*. We imagine that more time always equals more output. We hold our friends to that standard, and our children, and we hold ourselves to it, too. Yet that can't possibly be true. Because we don't live in an industrial age any more. Perhaps in a Victorian factory that was true (although I doubt it). But now so much of our work isn't about *what we do;* it's about *how we think*. And no one thinks better when they're only surviving on an extraordinary caffeine intake and three hours sleep. No one thinks better when their emotions are so fragile that the wrong text message, or the wrong comment from a friend or colleague, can send us into a downward spiral.

Today is Wednesday, the middle of the working week. The tipping point. The cobwebs from the weekend are gone, and thoughts haven't turned to whatever plans we have for the next one. It's a kind of equilibrium.

If you are interested, like me, in living the happiest and most productive life you can, then the idea of equilibrium, of balance, is worth thinking about. If we knew the perfect point of equilibrium in our energy levels, our point of balance, then perhaps – in the end – we could finally begin to trust it. Everyone's point of equilibrium is different, so I can't tell you what yours is. I can tell you that you need to look after yourself physically, mentally, emotionally and spiritually. And I can tell you this with almost complete certainty: you are working too hard. Take some time with someone you love. Get a hug. Read a book, even just for 20 minutes.

Give yourself a break.

Chapter Seven

Harder and Longer Aren't Always Best

Written on 23rd August, 2017

Here's where I'm dancing at the moment. I'm trying to release the link, ingrained in me, that more success only comes from working *harder* and working *longer*.

I know this isn't true. I know that I coach better when I'm rested, deeply in touch with myself, calm. And I know that working 60+ hours in a week, including late nights and early starts, doesn't help with my *actual work*. It helped me get here, and it might get me more clients in the short term, but it doesn't enable me to serve those clients as well, as powerfully, as magically, as when I'm deeply centred and out of my own head.

More than that, I know that when I get out of my head and let inspiration strike, great things happen. My most-read article poured out over two sittings. I had an idea to write it, but I didn't actually do that until a client cancelled at late notice. Then I sat there and checked in and said: '*What shall I do now, with this time?*' And the answer came: '*Get on with it and write that piece about how you got here.*'

I've been asking myself, recently, '*What next?*' I've reached my two-year dream, the last bit of vision for the future that I had in place. I've said to myself, '*I can't put time into creating something magical, because I don't know what it is.*' But the truth is, I can't find the magical thing until I give myself the space, and take the action, to let inspiration in.

So this is where I'm dancing, with help from my coach, and I set myself a task: create something just for you. Something at the edge of what I'm 'allowed' to create. Maybe just beyond that. And today I did. I sat down in a coffee shop in London and wrote. And every time I stopped writing, I sat back and opened myself and asked: '*What wants to be written?*' And then I wrote it.

This was a strange experience. I didn't know what was going to come. It was quite different to what I'd written before; more like some of my brother's writing, in some ways, than mine. But with my own spin, with ingredients of me. And something more. Something beyond me. I'm not sure if I'll publish it or if it's just for me. But what I do know is that I left the coffee shop feeling different. Having opened myself to inspiration, it came. And this afternoon I had a clearer head, clearer thoughts, and took more enjoyment – while being very productive – than I thought I would out of the things on my list. I replied to emails, wrote 80 per cent of a website about a project my friend Nicole and I are working on, and took part in a group call, stretching myself into question-asking territory. Good things will come from all these things.

Somehow, dancing in the space of inspiration, in Jim Dethmer's Through Me[1], comes productivity without *harder* and *longer*. Without the *pain* of *harder* and *longer*.

I'm not comfortable with this yet, I still have the fear. This week, I haven't had many coaching sessions or many meetings. I've joyed in the independence and freedom... about half the time. The rest of the time my fear has been loud: '*You need to do more, or you'll be poor and homeless.*'

But this week I have written, I have business-planned, I have reflected on my Zone of Genius; I have learnt, I have read, I have moved a project towards completion.

Any or each of those could lead to more success – however I choose to define it – than I could have got by emailing, calling or meeting any single potential client.

But how do we get comfortable with that? That's where I'm dancing.

Notes

1. As I wrote in *How to Start When You're Stuck*, the *Life Happening To Me/ Life Created By Me/ Life Happening Through Me/ Life Happening As Me* framework, which I first read about in Jim Dethmer, Diana Chapman and Kaley Warner Klemp's book, *The 15 Commitments of Conscious Leadership,* is a powerful tool for thinking about ourselves and how we are responding to life.

Chapter Eight

Balancing the Past, Present and Future

Written on 3rd March, 2017

We put ourselves through things, don't we? We sacrifice energy or time from the future for the present: doing things we know will make tomorrow that little bit harder, whether that thing is drinking wine, staying up later than we should, or even drinking coffee when we know that the caffeine crash will follow.

And we save our energy or our happiness up for the future, too. Working ourselves to the bone now so that in the future, at some point, we can finally relax and get what we want.

We know these days (or at least we are told from many angles) that living in the present moment will help us with anxiety, with stress, with pretty much everything.

So why is it that we put ourselves through pain today, for space tomorrow? Or through a rush of energy today, knowing the pain will come tomorrow?

Well, I think it's because we know, instinctively, the path for ourselves. Most of us aren't zen master Thich Nhat Hanh, living in the moment every moment (and maybe not even he is). But neither are we a hedonistic seventies rock star, wrecking all our tomorrows in pursuit of just one more moment of *that feeling*. Neither are we the imagined corporate slave, having their back broken by an awful employer, trying to fulfil their dream of retirement.

Most of us know there is a balance and we try and find it. We know the joy of an evening of four glasses of wine, and we know that even though tomorrow will be harder, it is worth it. And we know that sometimes you do have to set an intention for the future and work towards it, and *that* is worth it. And we know that to try and live in the moment is a powerful thing, that enjoying where we are is a part of almost every successful journey.

And we strive for that balance. The right one for us. We strive for it. To enjoy the moment, to take advantage of the amazing things that the 21st century offers, which aren't always good for us, and to transform our life into what we want.

It's not always easy to find the balance. But we strive for it.

Chapter Nine

The Struggle to Celebrate Success

Written on 9th December, 2016

Why do so many of us struggle to celebrate our success? It's an idea that I have wrestled with regularly in the last few years, as my path became clearer, and as I had more successes to celebrate as I started to move down it. And it's something that clients mention to me reasonably regularly. 'I achieve a goal, but then it's on to the next one' is a feeling I know only too well.

Tim Ferriss, on his excellent podcast, often asks his guests: 'When you think of the word "successful" who comes to mind?' The answers are fairly consistent. People either give an example of someone – almost always someone we all know – or they question the concept of success.

In a recent article he wrote, my brother Ewan Townhead explains that the origin of the word success is the same as that for succession. Something that comes after. Given the momentum that comes from that etymology, is it any wonder that by the time you have achieved your first goal, you are already thinking about the next one?

But celebrating the good things in your life is important. We all know it is. And as we learn more and more about psychology and neuroscience, it takes on even greater importance: the things we focus on are the things we notice more of, so focusing on the good things will help us notice more of them. And that's got to be good, right? Not only that, but in the ever-increasing pressure of the social media age, it can be so hard to remember that things are going well in our own life, when all the wonderful things in other people's are in our faces day after day. Celebrating the things that go well is an imperative if we want to increase our wellbeing.

So here are some suggestions:

- **Focus on the feeling you want, not the 'thing'.** This is what changed things for me. I want to feel brilliant. I want the buzz of energy running through me. And I want it as much as I can. And when I notice that, it's worth stopping and acknowledging that. It's worth celebrating.

- **Stop periodically.** One of the things that I have seen make the most difference to clients is to build a time to stop and celebrate into their life on a regular basis. I do it with my clients: pause with them to acknowledge when things have gone well. It changes the way they see the things they have going on.

- **When you notice it, share it with someone you love.** In person or on the phone is best, but email or a WhatsApp will do. A short, specific 'I'm pleased with this' or 'I feel great today' is enough.

But remember, this is a habit you have to build up. It won't happen overnight. Notice it, when you can. Change, when you notice.

Chapter Ten

The Friday Feeling of Freedom

Written on 11th November, 2016

I'm excited this morning. I woke up an hour before my alarm and couldn't sleep. Thoughts were running through my head, everything from the great Manchester United midfield three of Carrick, Scholes and Fletcher, to the work that might unfold for me in 2017, to – most of all – this weekend, when I am meeting a group of old friends. We are geographically scattered across the country, but are in touch every day by the magic of the communication age. We support each other, discuss current affairs, talk a lot about football, and provide a shot of energy, humour and community into each other's lives. We haven't had this many of us in the same room for years. It's going to be great.

As I ate my breakfast this morning, the sun pouring in through the windows of my new flat, I felt really excited. The world seemed open. No ideas were stupid. Everything had a positive frame. Anything could happen.

And that's when something clicked for me. I've had long running correspondence for something approaching a decade now with one of those friends about the Monday Feeling. How can we enjoy Mondays more? What causes that general misery that everyone recognises from some point in their life as being what happens on Mondays?

Over our years of experimentation, we've concluded that, for us and others, increased alcohol consumption at the weekend plays a part. My recent experiments with my diet have shown me that sugar (and the subsequent crash) plays a part, too. But this morning I got this flash, which goes a long way to completing the puzzle. And it comes from reframing the question to: why is the Friday Feeling so good?

And the answer is that on Friday, it feels like anything could happen. Not that anything could happen right now at this moment, necessarily, but it's coming: the weekend is here. There is a sense of freedom, of openness, of possibility.

I have been moving towards this thought over the last year, as I've worked for myself for about half the time, and for another organisation (and a lovely, caring one, I should add) about half the time.

No matter how great the work is that the organisation I work for does (it's great!), and no matter what a great place it is to work (it's great!), there is a real difference between being in total control of your life, from the tasks you do to the vision you have, that comes so much more easily when you work for yourself. And it's this sense of possibility. Of freedom. I believe this is pulling more and more people into freelance work, into contracting, and away from the traditional career path.

And as I look forward to this weekend, with this buzz in my chest and a smile on my face, I can't help but wonder: how can I get more of this feeling? And how can I give this feeling to others? And what would the world be like if everyone – in every home and workplace – had this feeling all of the time?

This buzz that comes from the instinct, the evolutionary drive, to make things happen, to see things change. This excitement. This freedom. This possibility.

When do you have it? And how can you create more?

Chapter Eleven

The Sweet Sadness of Beauty Never to Come Again

Written on 22nd March, 2019

I've noticed something about myself. There is a particular kind of sadness that it enriches my life to feel. Not deep sadness, and not panic or horror or tragedy. But the chance to feel sadness, on my behalf or someone else's, has a sweetness to it sometimes.

The tingle in the nose, the tears in the eyes. There is a freedom and an uplifting nature to it.

I once heard someone say that tears – and other emotions – are just another one of the body's ways of processing waste. We don't judge ourselves or others for going to the toilet, or having a snotty nose, so why should we judge ourselves or others for tears or anger or other emotions? These things are a fact of life.

I think that's right. Tears are a release of energy, and it is empowering and it is freeing to feel them. But more than that, it is a sign you are alive.

I love sadness, sweet sadness. I have for a long time. I once owned a t-shirt made by the band Lowgold, which said 'Keep Music Miserable' across my chest. My favourite TV show, probably, is *Six Feet Under* with its beautiful exposition of love, loss and emotion through experiences around death.

My favourite scenes in my favourite novels are more often than not the ones that bring tears to my eyes. But they are sweet tears. They are tears of heroism. They are tears of tragedy; of love, and love lost.

And the most memorable moments of my works as a coach are more often than not ones where there is a tingle in my nose and tears in my eyes as I sit, in connection with someone else, someone in a moment of heroism, or courage, or tragedy, or love. And they feel the tingle and the tears, too.

These are beautiful, enlivening, uplifting times. They are times, I've reflected before, where I feel my soul growing. And in some ways they have a sadness to them, a sweet sadness.

I don't like to cry in public, though. Even with my nearest and dearest it feels almost too private an experience: to feel my soul growing, and to touch a deeper truth about life.

And there is another reason for those tears, those moments of sweet sadness, to be in private. That is because another part of me, another value I hold dear, is one of solidity, of reliability, for those who need me. I'm here, I've got you, I'll be the one you can rely on.

But it is a vital and a joyous part of my life, sitting alone one morning, tears in my eyes at the noise of the children in the playground across the street. Or sitting one afternoon, turning the pages of the novel as the troubled soul finds redemption. Or watching, one evening, as the two cowboys decide to go down fighting: together, at the end, as friends. Or standing, one summer's day, witnessing love and openness shared in ceremony and in words, among loved ones.

These moments; they are life. Seek them out. Find them, where you can. Notice them. Savour them, for all the things they give to you, all the ways they change you.

This sweet sadness, at the beauty of humankind, which we see in a moment and then we lose, knowing that moment will never come again.

Chapter Twelve

The Importance of Time Alone

Written on 24th August, 2016

My girlfriend is away at the moment, on business in Singapore. Since she left I've been reflecting on two things that are stark: firstly, that I miss her a lot. She isn't there when I wake up in the morning. She isn't there to discuss the day with me (except in intermittent Skype calls at strange times when we overlap in being awake and available). She isn't there to eat with, to watch TV with, to do all those things that make up our life together. And secondly, she isn't there to give me the energy or the love that she does.

And yet, also, I like time by myself. I get a lot done, both in work and home life. But there is something more than that. I need time by myself. It allows all the parts of me to settle back to where they would naturally be. It is *restful*.

I enjoy the fact that my train has lots of other people on it but I also like turning my music up and drifting away.

Working with colleagues is a joy, but on my days working on my own business, I feel a sense of settling in my being which I don't get from someone else's aims, objectives and projects.

My life would be an immeasurably poorer place without Emma. But I am a better man, for her and for me, with that rest and that *settling* that only comes from time alone.

Chapter Thirteen

Replace Your Destructive Habits With Kindness

Written on 7th September, 2018

It takes commitment to change. It always has, and it always will.

Steven Pinker, in his fascinating book *The Better Angels of Our Nature: A History of Violence and Humanity*, talks about the process of civilisation being one of resisting our natural, animal instincts. Each time we resist our baser instincts, we move further from the incredibly brutal history of our race, into the far more peaceful and safer world that we (and by 'we' I mean almost certainly all of the people reading this) currently inhabit.

For those of us lucky enough to live in Western Europe (as well as in many other nations around the world), over generations our societies have given us the opportunity to live more and more from our higher selves – our creative, ingenious, loving selves – and less and less from our baser instincts, those where we cause pain and destruction, even in small ways, for ourselves and others.

I was reading recently about changing habits: that the best way to change a habit is to replace it with a different habit. (Interestingly, the writer, Steve Chandler, said the difficulty of changing a habit is not affected by the length of time you have had that habit, but that's another story.) Today, as I considered some of the exchanges and vitriol that happen in our society (it may or may not surprise you that I was checking Twitter at the time), and also some of the times my baser instincts emerge, I considered creating a new habit. It was helped along – as many parts of my thinking are – by the words of singer-songwriter Frank Turner, whose latest album is titled *Be More Kind*.

Here is the thought that came to mind. What would happen if, every time I felt myself shifting into the kind of person I don't want to be – in particular, when I feel my anger and irritation rising to the point where I may cause pain and hurt, and I find myself lashing out with words – I leaned, instead into kindness? And further, what would happen if each of us committed that each time we find ourselves on the edge of being critical or hurtful or destructive, we instead took a breath and thought: 'Wait. Instead, how can I be more kind?'

The question is one I like: this is not necessarily about being perfectly kind; it is about being *more* kind. Resisting that instinct just a little more than we would have otherwise. Making a small change. Each time. Except the times when we don't, of course, when we slip in our commitment. Then we just need to recommit.

And then each of us, resisting those baser instincts and behaviours, and leaning into our more loving, creative, kinder, higher selves, will take the whole world that little step further into civilisation.

Because that's how change works. It doesn't work by someone declaring something from on high, or even from a referendum result or an election. It works when many, many normal, ordinary people like you and I take a stand in our lives. For example, when each of us, every day, is more kind.

Chapter Fourteen
Drugs, Organising and Thermodynamics

Written on 15th June, 2018

The laws of physics creep into our lives even when we don't notice it. The first law of thermodynamics is: energy is conserved, it cannot be created or destroyed. I was reminded this week how true that is in our lives.

Steve Chandler writes regularly about his experiences with addiction and recovery. It was Steve, in one of his articles, who introduced me to the idea that when we take drugs, we are often borrowing from the future. Even the drugs we consume every day or week have this effect. Just think what happens when you drink a cup of coffee or a glass of wine. A rush of energy. And what happens later: an energetic low. Unless we consume more of the drug, in which case we borrow *more* from the future, and later we pay even more back. Sometimes we may not notice, we may pay it back by getting worse sleep, again borrowing very subtly from future days.

It's more than just energy that I borrow from the future, particularly with alcohol. I borrow self-assurance, and confidence. I borrow charm. I borrow the ability to think.

I borrow belief that things will turn out right. And in the following days, those things are conspicuous by their absence from my life.

When I drink coffee in the morning, I joy in the rush of excitement about life, and energy. I love it as I read, or coach, or create. And then later, in the afternoon or early evening, I pay it back, with those things conspicuous by their absence from my life.

I am in the midst of organising my wedding. I am not finding this particularly fun. My friend Cat told me she *hated* the build up to her wedding. And then the day itself – the culmination of months of doing things she hated – was one of the most amazing times in her life. It occurred to me that Cat was lending fun and energy to the future – as Emma and I are now – in a strange reversal of the experience of alcohol.

I am sacrificing doing things now that would be more fun: watching the World Cup, reading, watching my favourite series on Netflix, literally *anything* other than organising (or sometimes it feels like that). And in exchange, I will get a day which I can see will be a truly special day. It is taking my energy, my contentment, my happiness, my joy now (although sometimes it gives me some, too). And I trust – through the experiences of others, and as I see the day that is coming together – that it will be a day which will pay back that energy, contentment, happiness and joy in one amazing 18-hour flash.

I didn't like my work as much when it was almost solely about organising. I used to organise events, plays, concerts, youth theatre performances. Later, I organised transformational training experiences. I decided I couldn't spend my life pouring my energy into that. Now I see that was because I wasn't present for many of those events: I didn't get the pay back of energy I was putting in. But it was still conserved. It was passed to audience members, young performers, and later leaders.

In my life, I don't mind this too much. I prefer a life of highs and lows – as long as the lows aren't too low – to one of steadiness. Life is about love, last minutes and lost evenings, after all. But in my work, it was important to receive the energy back for the things I create. That's the only sustainable way. The only way I could be sure I could keep going.

So be careful with yourself. Notice the people, the places, the things you do that only take your energy: where you pass it on to them, to there, to that, and don't receive it back. Or you don't receive it back soon enough to keep going.

Be careful of the things that used to pay back at other times in our history. Worries and fears and anxiety take energy from the present. Our ancestors would be paid back by staying alive, while those who hadn't lent energy to the future by worrying died. Worry and fear take up an enormous amount of our energy and that is a price worth paying when your life is at stake. But mostly – and we should count ourselves lucky about this – our lives aren't at stake when we worry and fear these days. And that sacrifice of energy, of happiness, of time, of joy may not be worth it.

The message here is this: be aware when you are borrowing or lending energy from or to the future, or to someone else. Then make a choice.

Chapter Fifteen

Our Body Knows More Than We Think, and Thinks More Than We Know

Written on 2nd November, 2018

A client was late for a session this morning.

I have a practice that whenever someone is late, or cancels a session at late notice, I don't just dive into my inbox. Instead, I do something cool instead. Or something awesome. Or something exciting. Or something creative. My most-read article was mostly written after a client cancelled at the last minute. Thank you – from me, and on behalf of the 7,500 people who have read it – to the client that cancelled.

Today, I reflected on a workshop I went on with Loch Kelly, an author and teacher of Effortless Mindfulness. At the workshop, the most powerful of the glimpse-practices he taught – ways to glimpse a different kind of awareness without having to spend many years practising meditation – was one that included movement. I have only used it once since the workshop, so in the 15 minutes I had, I did the practice three times, using a four-minute video Kelly has posted on YouTube. Something about the movement Kelly took me through at the workshop and in the video connects me to my awareness and alters my state better than any other of his practises.

And this doesn't surprise me. One of my journeys of the last few years has been to lean into and deepen my understanding of my body. I feel this has the power to unlock wonders for me in my work and life, with signs coming to me from all angles.

I remember first reading about the psychology experiment where participants are instructed to hold the muscles in their face in the form of a smile (without being told to smile). They report being happier. If they are instructed to hold their facial muscles in a sad expression, they report feeling sadder.

It's not just that, though. I've written elsewhere about the centring exercise I do before every coaching session. One of my clients has an aim to be more present in the evenings with her family and I gave her the same exercise to trial on her commute home. The first part of the exercise is to stand in a physically centred position: feet flat, shoulders above hips, back straight but not overextended, to breathe deeply and to breathe out tension. The exercise goes on into a kind of mindfulness practice but she reported that *just by changing her posture* she felt calmer.

Jordan Peterson, in his book *12 Rules For Life*, talks about how the one of the effects of the dominance hierarchy that humans (and, memorably, lobsters) have evolved as part of the way we organise ourselves, is that we get into positive and negative feedback loops and part of this is posture. If we stand up straight, with our shoulders back, then our body gives us hormones which support us feeling better, even making better decisions. Not only that, but people treat us better, which gives us even more of the good hormones. If we slump and slouch, instead, then we get hormones which tell us things won't work out, things won't be easy, they won't be possible. And people treat us in a way that encourages more of that. And as more of those hormones come in, we slouch even more.

When I am preparing myself for coaching, I have noticed that changing the position of my arms affects how I feel enormously. Out to my sides and up makes it harder to breathe. Down and curved out, with palms up, seems to welcome energy into me.

Psychologist Ellen Langer says that the distinction of Body and Mind is arbitrary. There is no separation. It might as well, she memorably says, have been Mind, Body and Elbow. A group of people in one of the experiments she talks about act younger, live in an environment made to look like several decades ago, and then start to *look younger*. Isn't that extraordinary?

The message of this article is simple. Your body holds great intelligence, it holds great intuition, and it affects how you think and how you feel. And vice versa.

Bring some more awareness to your body now. What do you notice?

Chapter Sixteen

Four Lessons from the Freedom of Creation

Written on 30th April, 2018

I clear my mind. Well, a little, anyway. I clear it to see what emerges in this, my first time writing on the train for a while. And then it gets a little less clear because I forget to keep it clear and read some emails instead.

These pieces, written in 12 minutes or so, were an exercise. An exercise in creation, and beating Resistance. And also an exercise in freedom. What if there's no time to think, and there's only time to create? What would happen then?

And, surprisingly, things happen. Things are created. Sometimes they end up being read 800 times, sometimes less than 20.

And, with a breath, and a recommitment to the freedom of creation, what will emerge today?

- **Nature has a strange effect on us.** It reconnects us to us. I don't know why that is, but nature is almost always a route to presence, to the real, unadulterated, honest you. And me. It is invigorating. *Seek it more.*

- **A collection of people carries an energy.** Maybe one day we'll find the science behind it – some tiny particle which means that a group of people *feel* collectively. So a crowd of unruly, joyful children lead us to feeling one way, and a crowd of worn out commuters lead us to feeling a different way. Pay attention to this. *Notice the people around you.*

- **It's scary to be vulnerable**. It feels like there are people we can't be vulnerable with. But the truth is that by not being vulnerable with those people we just – almost all the time – make being vulnerable seem more scary. And, almost all the time, if we leaned into vulnerability just a few more per cent, we would learn that actually it's safe to be a little more vulnerable. A little more open. A little more us. So lean that way. *Give yourself a chance to be brave, a chance to learn that you can.*

- **The answers are always within.** It's so hard to see this, but deep inside us are the answers to almost all of our wants, our 'needs', our suffering, our ambitions and our struggles. I can't always see this. Sometimes I know it deeply, sometimes I 'know it' intellectually, but I can't feel it at all. But I believe it, I think. Most of the time. So try it, when you can. *Look inside when you need answers.*

Chapter Seventeen

The Cycles That Help You Flourish

Written on 15th February, 2019

Two people talked to me this week about some new ideas about sleep. Apparently, it's not the number of hours you get that matters. Because sleep is about cycles, and what matters over the course of the week is the number of *sleep cycles* you get.

And life is like that.

I came back from holiday this week. I spent Monday and Tuesday and most of Wednesday feeling that beautiful recharged, relaxed feeling that I love to have, and that time off work often gives me. Then on Wednesday afternoon or evening, something shifted. I spent Thursday feeling different: edgy, anxious, wondering, worrying. Tired.

This morning, things feel different again. I feel alive, awake, calm, relaxed, recharged. I have a smile on my face as I write this.

That's one of my cycles: relaxed/recharged – edgy/anxious – relaxed/recharged.

Life isn't quite like sleep, though. Because it's not about how many cycles you can get in in a week. Life is about how quickly you can move through the parts of your cycles that stop you from flourishing.

I spoke to a client about it this morning. My suspicion is that all of us, even the Dalai Lama, go through cycles like the one I've just described. But the Dalai Lama (and other incredibly relaxed, calm people) are *really* good at moving through the edgy/anxious phase fast. So fast. Perhaps even in a single moment. Perhaps, in the end, so fast that they don't even notice it is there. But remember, they are human, too. Just like I am. Just like you are.

My friend Kate Rees does work on resilience: she told me it's not about not suffering or struggling. Resilience is about how quickly you bounce back.

That's what Brené Brown says, too. We all get knocked down, she says. What is interesting is what sets apart the people who flounder after the knocks from those who rise strong.

So what are the things that help us to bounce back, to rise strong, to move through the difficult parts of the cycle? There are so many and different ones will help at different times. But here are the ones that emerge from me in this moment. Play with them. Choose some to experiment with this week.

Eat well.

Always assume the best of people.

Ask, 'How could I be wrong?'

Sleep well.

Speak about what has happened to you.

Keep a journal.

Don't trust your feelings, they aren't always right.

Don't trust your thoughts, they aren't always right.

Be grateful for what you have.

Listen more to others.

Listen less to the voice in your head. You know the one. Don't listen to it. It might have been useful once, and it might mean well, but it's not helping you to flourish.

Gift yourself something: some thing or time or activity that speaks to your soul.

Spend time in nature.

Sing.

Hold someone close.

Allow yourself to be held.

Smile at a stranger.

Be kind.

Be vulnerable.

Help someone else.

Compare yourself not to others today, but to yourself yesterday.

This last one is perhaps the most important. Remember how long it used to take you to get through the most difficult parts of your cycles. My guess is it used to take longer yesterday – and even longer many yesterdays ago – than it does today. That's great. That's because you've been doing your work.

If you want to make it even shorter, then that's a good ambition. That's the route to a life of flourishing. If that's the case, maybe we should talk. Because that's the work. That's the important work that we should all be doing.

Part Two: CREATE THE PEOPLE AND RELATIONSHIPS YOU NEED

If you had asked me 10 years ago how to create the conditions for great work, I'm not sure how clear I would have been. But I suspect I could have guessed that there would be some things we need to do (Part One) and with my interest in psychology growing, I might have guessed that there were ways we need to think (Part Three).

But I doubt very much I would have talked about relationships. In Part Two you will find ideas, ways of thinking and – I hope – inspiration to create the relationships you need in order to thrive.

I have a tendency towards what psychologist and author Robert Holden calls dysfunctional independence. As Holden says, each new level of success requires a new level of partnership.

The chapters that follow show you how I thought about and wrestled with that over these three years, trying to find and create the support I needed to do my best work. Toni Morrison said: 'If there's a book you really want to read, but it hasn't been written yet, then you must write it.' Whilst I didn't consciously set out to do that, undoubtedly this is what I did. Of all the parts of these books, this is among those I need to come back to over and over again; one of the most 'work-in-progress' for me. And one of the parts I'm most surprised emerged as a vital part of the process.

In it you'll find frames for thinking about the people around you, practices I think are vital for the relationships that *really* help us thrive, appreciation for the power of connection and what two or more people can do together, and more.

I hope from it you'll be reminded, as I am writing this, how much I stand on the shoulders of giants. Giants of the past, yes, but also those giants in my life: the partners, loved ones, family and friends who make this possible.

But it isn't enough to acknowledge that; we have to remember that we can create it. That in any relationship is the possibility for more. That anything, from a four-second hug to speaking about something you feel unable to speak about, can create more in our relationships. More of what we need, that is, if we are to be all that we can be.

If we want to create the conditions for great work, we can't do it alone.

Chapter Eighteen

The Three Groups of People You Need on Your Journey

Written on 11th June, 2019

Sometime last year my brother Ewan shared an idea with me. I think he heard it on a Tim Ferriss interview, but I can't remember who said it and I can't find it now. It went something like this:

If we are on a journey – say, of growth, or towards more success – we need three groups of people in our life.

First, we need people ahead of us on the journey. They may be the people we aspire to be like. The people we admire. And they have a vital function. They show us *it can be done*.

Second, we need people alongside us on the journey. They are the peers that show us we aren't going insane. That whatever we are going through is normal. They push us on to what is next, commiserate about the struggles and drive us on to even greater heights. They show us *we are not alone*.

But Ewan told me the story because of the third group. They were the group I hadn't thought of.

I was going a little mad at time. I was working with Rich Litvin – a member of the first group, for me – on one of his group coaching programmes that contained seven other amazing coaches who, on my best days, I knew were part of the second group. But the stress of this, of being in a group of people pushing themselves (and being pushed and pulled along by Rich), made life *hard* for me. Really hard. Until I went along to a meeting of a network of coaches I'm part of. And in the space of an hour or so I *relaxed*.

We need people who are behind us on the journey. They show us we have made progress. That we are doing well. That we are doing better than we were yesterday. They are not people we look down on; they are people whose journey and struggles we empathise with, but they make us realise that the work we are doing is *working*. They tell us, when we see them: 'You're not *here* any more. You're moving.' They tell us *we're doing ok*.

Those three groups are powerful. You might, like me, be missing one of these in your life. If you are, seek them out. You may not need them all the time, but a shot of each every now and again can make all the difference.

The first group will stretch you into the future, will help you as you envision what *could be*. Sit for a moment, and think of someone you deeply admire. Write out their qualities. Remember the lessons of shadow work: in order to admire qualities in someone – truly admire them – you have to deeply understand them. You can only do this if you have the spark of those qualities in you somewhere. *You could be the person you admire.*

The second group will ground you in the present, in your deep humanity. Find some others on the same journey as you. They might be colleagues in the same profession. They might be others who seek out a similar learning opportunity. They might be others setting out on the same adventure as you – perhaps marriage, or having children, perhaps changing career, or travelling the world. *There are others out there.*

The third group will remind you of Jordan Peterson's lesson on comparison in *12 Rules For Life*: compare yourself to you of the past, not others today. That's what that third group give you: you used to be like this, in some way, earlier on your quest. Have deep compassion for those people. Help them along however you can. But remember: you are not the you of yesterday. You have more capability, more space, more strength, more grace.

And all that work, all those struggles, all the suffering, all the triumph, all the tragedy... All of it has made a difference. To you, to those around you, and to the world.

Chapter Nineteen

The Three Kinds of Thinkers You Need to Improve Your Thinking

Written on 19th June, 2019

In the last chapter, I wrote about three groups of people you need with you on your journey, to help you stay on the path of growth towards whatever success you are following. That got me thinking about the kinds of people you need to have around you in order to think well, and continue to think even better and more clearly as time goes on. Here's what I came up with.

People who know less than you. It struck me, thinking about this, that maybe sometimes we do need to remember that we know a lot more about something than other people. I sometimes joke with 'new coaches' I work with that just by starting a coaching business they have thought about coaching more than at least 99 per cent of the people on the planet.

For me, this shows up less when I'm thinking about my business these days and more when I'm thinking about complex, important ideas: about politics, about government, about morality, about the environment, about how the world works. If you're interested in doing this thinking, it's incredibly easy in the internet age to think that you know nothing, because if you're like me you read articles by people who know *a lot* more than you, and you listen to those people, and you follow those people on Twitter, too. And we compare what's going on for us on the inside when we think about these ideas (in my case doubt, questioning, exploration, unsureness) with what's going on for other people on the outside (on Twitter, A LOT of certainty!), and we fall into a comparison trap. So we need some people around us who just haven't learnt about things as much as we have. Perhaps try seeking them out, or remind yourself of all the learning you have done about whatever it is you're thinking about.

People who disagree with you. The world *needs* disagreement. That's what our legal system rests on: people arguing their sides and a third passing judgment. It's what academia *should* rest on (although with things like the Grievance Studies fiasco, and narrowing political viewpoints on campus, it may be that not all of it does any more): academics putting their ideas out there, trusting that others will keep them honest and in check so that we can trust that studies that come out of academia are true.

Now this bit is *hard* to do in your personal life, but it is important, if you want to search for truth. As Jordan Peterson says in *12 Rules For Life,* when we debate things in our heads, we mostly construct quite idiotic opponents to do this with. If you want to improve your thinking, you need something more sophisticated. And luckily, most real people who have thought about the world are more sophisticated than the straw men and women we construct in our minds. But, having a disagreement in the modern era is difficult. People aren't good at it, or at least aren't doing it with good humour. If we don't do it with good humour and while assuming the best of the other and giving them the benefit of the doubt, we shout people down and we shut people down. That's why so many of us feel unable to speak about so many things. This is why it's important that when *you* disagree with someone, you do it with good humour, you assume the best of them and you give them the benefit of the doubt. And you don't shout them down.

And that's why we need the third group. **We need people with whom we agree**, or at least with whom we can explore our ideas, excitedly, out further than we have ever explored before. We need thinking partners. That's what my friend Colin Smith does. He calls himself the Listener, but really people don't pay him to listen; they pay him to help them think better than they have ever done before. That's what I do in my coaching, too. That's what Rebel Wisdom did, miraculously, at their summit this year: they created thinking partnerships between total strangers by curating the conversation beautifully.

With a thinking partner you explore your thoughts, without judgment. They may know about the idea, or they may just have the skills to open conversations and pursue thinking in an unusual way. You explore together: your thinking then goes up and out into new places. Of course that's also why we need the challenge sometimes from the second group, to make sure that what we are saying is grounded in reality. But it is a wonderful and (in my experience) rare thing to have true thinking partners. I'm lucky to have them in my family, and I love those conversations as we explore ideas and say things we couldn't say almost anywhere else, with curiosity. It's why I pay someone (my coach) to listen to me, to be my thinking partner, to help me take my ideas up and out into possibility.

Make sure to find some spaces in your life to remember the qualities your thinking already has, perhaps with some people who haven't thought about things as much as you have. Be kind and curious as you do this.

Make sure you find some spaces in your life to be challenged, to be kept honest, to be outside the echo chamber. But find ones who will give you the benefit of the doubt, and give the benefit of the doubt to others.

And make sure you have people around you who can support your thinking, who can help you take it above and beyond what you thought possible.

Chapter Twenty

What Do You Feel Unable to Speak About?

Written on 20ᵗʰ May, 2019

I went to an event last week that met a need in me I had barely realised was there. Well, that's not quite true. I had realised it was there, but I hadn't realised what a difference it would make to me to be able to have that need met.

I attended the Rebel Wisdom Summit, an all-day event run by an organisation (started as a YouTube channel) who believe there is a sense-making crisis and a meaning-making crisis in the world and host conversations and events to try to help the world work through that. The event featured four fascinating speakers, including Brett Weinstein and Heather Heying, who in some quarters are famous for the fascinating events at Evergreen College in the USA where what seemed a fairly simple and straightforward interaction between Weinstein and other faculty escalated into some fairly frightening scenes with students' behaviour becoming threatening and, to many outside the university sector, outrageous. But more than the speakers, something else was important: Rebel Wisdom did something really special.

They created a space, primed in various ways, where *curiosity* and *giving people the benefit of the doubt* was the default position. I hadn't realised how little I feel that is the case, especially when modern social issues are discussed.

One of the exercises we undertook, in small groups (and in the afternoon, once we had had a chance to create an environment of trust), was to allow each member of the group three minutes to answer the question: 'What do you feel unable to speak about?' Take a moment, if you like, to think about what you might speak about. I imagine for most people, like me, there may be quite a list of possibilities.

What transpired in that exercise was something really beautiful, which was the moment when my unmet need was met: people spoke beautifully, calmly and passionately about things that matter, things that affect our society and our world. And they spoke with nuance. *And no one jumped down anyone's throat.* No one started calling 'racist' or 'fascist'. When people shared something that might sound strange to others, those listening had an internal reaction – I could feel this happening for me, and see it for others – but then a settling of curiosity and of benefit of the doubt: *that sounds a little odd, but I'm going to sit with this and see where they're going.*

For a long time I've been someone who likes to look for the truth. I have always deeply believed in right and wrong, and I know that that means sometimes speaking up or saying the difficult things. My favourite scene in the work of my favourite author involves a man doing something heroic – doing what is right – even though he has no chance of success, because it is *the right thing to do*. That interest in the truth means I hold nuanced views – which I have thought about *a lot* – on things that certain people would find difficult to hear. They are things I don't feel able to talk about in most company, because I fear I would be labelled a racist for holding nuanced views on immigration, or be labelled a transphobe for having nuanced views on the trans rights conversation. I have been labelled a 'denier' (a loaded term with deliberate holocaust connotations) by my boss, no less, at an organisation I used to work in because of my nuanced views on climate change.

This does happen and has happened and it isn't nice. And it happens everywhere. And it keeps people quiet, and it stops important conversations from happening.

Wow, it was a relief to have those conversations, to be able to assume that the people there were likely to listen to you, to be curious about why you hold views, even when you are saying something they disagree with. I didn't know how much I needed that space, but I did.

To change the way the world works, we need to take a stand for truth, for meaning, for sense-making. To do that, we need to have conversations. To do that, we have to do two things. *We have to assume that others are doing their best, that they are trying to work all this stuff out, just like we are.*

And *we have to be brave*. We have to speak up, even when our out-dated nervous system slips into fight or flight, thinking we are actually going to die if we are pushed out of the group. We have to tell the truth, as we see it.

It's not easy, but it's important.

Chapter Twenty-One

To Learn, We Need to Give People the Space to Speak

Written on 23rd November, 2018

I've never been very good at speaking out when I disagree with people. I don't know exactly when it started or why, but I remember arriving at university to find a bunch of people who spoke incredibly confidently about things. So confidently that I didn't disagree. I was never as sure about anything as they were. There were too many other perspectives I knew I hadn't seen, and there was too much knowledge in the world that I didn't know. They must have just seen more perspectives, I thought, or have learned more. They probably had, in some cases, but later I realised that wasn't necessarily true. Sometimes, they just knew how to speak with self-assuredness, even on things about which they knew very little. On one occasion, an incredibly self-assured friend of mine denied that there were any selective schools in the UK. She was so self-assured that I almost didn't correct her, and so self-assured that when she at first denied it, I doubted myself – despite the fact that there were two selective secondary schools in the next school district over from the one I grew up in!

There's nothing inherently bad about this self-assured-ness: it's a useful tool – especially as many of us often find ourselves outside our comfort zone – to be able to sound more confident than you feel. But this period at university was the first time I remember it feeling oppressive. I didn't want to speak up to friends like that one, because I would be shouted down and the argument wouldn't be worth having: I wouldn't know the answer for sure and they would think they did, so what was the point? I wasn't up for the fight. This might be out of a fear of being wrong or a fear of losing an argument or something different altogether. But the feeling was oppressive.

I've been thinking about that again recently. I've spent a lot of time this week in the company of the moral psychologist Jonathan Haidt. His work – on our political and moral make up, and now on what he calls 'the coddling of the American mind' – is so interesting that I went to three events he was speaking at this week. One of the things he is talking about, in his talks and in his latest book, is a 'call-out' culture developing in American universities. It seems, from the questions at the events, that something similar is happening in UK universities. In my experience, this is not limited to academia.

What a 'call-out' culture is, as I understand it, is a culture where if someone uses the wrong word (often a word that might be offensive to some), or makes a mistake, or phrases something wrong, or says something that might be considered, say, racist, then they are called out. But the atmosphere as this is done is not one of learning. It is not one of 'did you perhaps make a mistake there?' or 'did you know someone might find that word offensive?' It is one, for the one being called out, of being oppressed. It is one where the call-out involves labelling the person. Perhaps they are labelled a racist, whether they actually are or not, and often when they are clearly not. One woman at an event I was at this week was accused in a petition – in advance of a lecture she was giving at King's College London – of being opposed to the wellbeing *and survival* of, among other groups, women.

Stories like this remind me of that feeling of being oppressed I used to feel at university. I've felt it more recently, too. Times when friends or colleagues or people at an event say something that I feel is wrong. 'But,' I think, 'it's not worth saying anything here. I might be called out. I might be labelled as something.' It's really, really unpleasant to be labelled as something you are not, especially something that your values are very much set against.

Why am I writing about this? What's the problem here? Well, the problem with that university culture, which may be spreading out more broadly, is the same as my conversation with my friend about school systems. If you create a dynamic and an environment where people feel it's not worth sharing their views because they might be shouted down, then learning can't occur. Whether that's shouted down by a slightly-too-self-assured and slightly-too-good-at-arguing friend, or by the kind of people who try to hound speakers off campus by essentially slandering them with baseless (and quite ridiculous) accusations. Either way, it stops learning. It stops understanding developing. It stops us finding the truth.

To learn – and we all need to learn about each other in this connected world we live in – we have to give everyone the space and environment where they can share the truth, as they see it.

Chapter Twenty-Two

Why is Some Feedback Hard to Take?

Written on 26ᵗʰ April, 2017

Recently, someone pointed out to me a kind of tick I sometimes have. It's a particular kind of in-breath that I sometimes take, sharply, often through my teeth. I think I do it when I'm asked a question I don't know the answer to and am buying myself time. In this case, it was even more noticeable than usual because it was happening into a microphone over a Skype call.

She followed this up by asking if anyone had mentioned this to me before. And at this point, I lied, or mumbled something about 'maybe' or 'people have said something like that'. Now I don't often lie, and I'm not often that flustered by something, so this got me curious.

And I reflected on it a few times in the next few days. Noticing the feeling of discomfort that came up, repeatedly, when I remembered it. Trying to spot it in my everyday speech. Suddenly becoming more aware of *all* my verbal ticks: all the 'so's, and 'kind of's, and 'really's that fit in around my words.

Not all feedback throws me like this, so why did this make such an impact? And why does pointing out someone's ticks often have such an impact? Because I've seen it in more than one friend or colleague in the past. And why does it not matter a jot to me when my coach tells me about any number of strange and wonderful things that I do, from the way I talk, to the expressions I have, to everything in between? And why can my supervision group talk quite openly about my coaching, which is so important to me, without leaving me lost in my head like this observation about a sharply taken in-breath had?

And I should say, this feedback was kindly given by a charming woman. And she gave it to help me prepare for recording a video: she was helping and it was helpful.

Well, here are my thoughts. Feedback hurts and confuses us when we feel *judged*. But particularly when we feel ourselves, our actual unique selves, are being judged. At that point, we feel that the core of our being, built over many years and decades, is being pointed at. And we're being told to change it. Because our speech patterns are so much a part of us. So much a key part of how we show the world who we really are. I felt like I was being told that I wasn't good enough. I needed to be changed to be accepted. And without the trust and love that I have for my coach and my supervision group, even when delivered reasonably skilfully, that hurts.

So be careful with your feedback. It hurts when we feel *who we are* is being judged. And when we don't feel enough trust to hear the love behind that feedback.

Chapter Twenty-Three

Sometimes, Say Exactly What You Mean

Written on 15th March, 2019

One of my favourite moments of coaching never actually happened. I was a member of a group of coaches – learning together – and we played a game. Someone shared a situation they were dealing with and each coach offered them a question. The person sharing then got to choose which question to answer.

The person in question – let's call them the client – had been speaking about the challenges of having their Left Brain and Right Brain in conflict. Another coach gave a beautiful intervention, which made me laugh and almost applaud because of its elegance: 'Can you tell us the situation again but without using the word "brain"?'

The client chose to answer a different question but I have remembered that moment ever since, because that question unlocked for me something I had seen in the client but been unable to articulate. The phrases 'left brain' and 'right brain' were holding her back. They didn't give us – the listeners – the full detail of what they meant (I'm still not sure I remember the difference); they assumed that we knew. But also, in this case, it felt to me – and the coach who asked the question – that they didn't give *the speaker* the full detail of what she meant. That unpacking them would be of huge benefit to her.

Language is a fascinating thing, and the words we use matter. As phrases pass into common parlance, they provide us with a wonderful way of short-cutting a repetitive explanation. We see this as we use acronyms in our offices; we see it in our daily life when we use phrases like 'work-life balance' or 'left wing' or 'vaping'. They have meanings. We know what they mean and they speed up and simplify conversations. That's one of the beauties of language, and if you try and imagine how life could possibly work without that process and those shortcuts it's basically impossible. These phrases and this evolution of language enable conversation and understanding to progress so much faster than it would otherwise.

Except when it doesn't.

Except when they slow down our thinking because they aren't able – in certain situations – to give the texture necessary to advance conversation and understanding. Except when they lead to misunderstandings, sometimes deliberately and sometimes accidentally. Or they lead to conversations being shut down, dialogue and debate silenced.

We pick these words and phrases up from popular culture and we use them. And they are useful. *And* it pays to slow down sometimes, to explain them, to expand them.

Sometimes we use them with careful understanding and sometimes we use them because we hear other people use them, or because they are used almost ideologically by 'people like me' (whether 'people like me' is 'coaches', 'conservatives', 'Remainers' or any other group).

Take this thought with you in the next few days or weeks. When are the shortcuts and phrases you use shutting down a conversation or a train of thought and when are they helping? Try replacing 'lean in' or 'political correctness gone mad' or 'fascist' with whatever you *actually mean* by that in this moment. And understand it will be different to what someone else means by that.

Notice it with others. When do *they* use a phrase and you don't quite know what they mean by it; when you wonder if *they* know what they mean? Notice it, particularly, if someone uses a phrase like this to shut down a conversation or make you feel small. It's basically impossible to increase understanding if we don't both know *exactly* what we mean.

Not all the time, of course.

But if you believe that we are living in more divided times, then asking that question – 'What exactly do you mean by that?' – with genuine curiosity, could be the way to open dialogues, change debates, and deepen our collective understanding.

And if you want to strengthen a relationship, the courage to say 'I don't know what that means', could be the vulnerability that allows for greater trust and intimacy, that allows genuine engagement, and that helps everybody learn.

Chapter Twenty-Four
The Four-Second Hug

Written on 19th May, 2017

Our physical condition plays a huge part in our lives and we need to remember that. I'm unwell at the moment and it has shaken my routine, so much so that I only remembered that this is my last trip into Central London of the week – and so my last opportunity to write a post – when I was part-way into my journey.

I have a heavy head cold. Nothing serious. I'm a man, though, so it has the added 'man flu' element, something I can only describe to those who don't get it as an evolutionary instinct of extreme frustration that *I don't work properly*. I imagine that there was real value in this frustration in past ages when people's – and particularly men's – livelihoods depended so much more on physical condition. *'Don't get ill!'* the evolutionary instinct shouts, and *'don't get injured!'*

But this is still important today, when my physical condition plays – in theory at least – a much smaller part in my livelihood. Those who exercise regularly will know the effect it has upon them afterwards. And not just the physical effect: the psychological and emotional effects that exercise – and indeed man flu frustration – can have across our lives.

I saw John Gray, famous for his seminal book, *Men Are From Mars, Women Are From Venus*, speak last week. If you haven't read that book, I highly recommend it, even 20 years on. The message from his hilarious and meandering talk was this: our hormones play a huge part in our relationships. This is a fact. And there are many and myriad ways of managing this and helping those we love reap the benefits of the hormone balances that are most advantageous to their happiness, growth, and fulfilment.

Sometimes I think we forget that. We think that if we just power through our tiredness or stress we will be ok. We might, but we might not, and who knows what happens to us in the meantime as we push and push and push.

So look after yourself. Find the ways to give yourself, physiologically and emotionally, what you need. And give it to those around you. You can, according to Dr Gray, start with a hug, four seconds long, for someone you care about. Four a day of these could transform the life of the woman you love by helping her hormone levels.

And if we can do that for others, what might we also be able to do for ourselves?

Chapter Twenty-Five

Criticism and Appreciation: How to Transform Your Intimate Relationships

Written on 25th July, 2018

I once heard an expert on relationships describe criticism as abuse. I have heard many people speak of criticism as the scourge of our intimate relationships. Last week, as I was re-listening to Alison Armstrong's *Understanding Women* programme, I heard more clearly than before why criticism is such a powerful and important part of what drives us apart in our relationships. Alison is an inspiration, whose research on men has left many men – including me – feeling more understood than they ever have before in their life. Her work about understanding women is important, too, and has opened up a far deeper understanding and appreciation in me for the women in my life.

At the heart of Armstrong's work is questioning the assumption many of us make that someone of the opposite sex is the same as someone of our own (perhaps women seeing a man as a hairy woman – often misbehaving – and men seeing women as over-emotional men). Questioning this assumption is certainly key in the way she talks about criticism.

One of the survival methods of women, as the mostly physically weaker members of the species, is to be incredibly adaptable. For much of our history, women needed men to physically protect them from the dangers of our environment. Some might argue that there are many occasions in the modern world, too, where the physically stronger among us could do with standing up a little bit more. This adaptability – and a long-standing emotional need, carried by the cavewoman in many of you – means that you respond to criticism. It changes you, to keep you safe. This doesn't mean that it's good, or it changes you in a good way, but it does change you. And this causes problems in a relationship.

Because criticism can have such a changing effect on a woman, she may sometimes use criticism to try to change a man. She does this from an incredibly well-meaning place: it may be that the criticism would be leading him towards being a better person, or a better partner, or even towards him being happier. But here's the problem: criticism doesn't change men. It only creates distance. It only pushes him away, with a message of 'it's not safe to be here, she doesn't want me as I am'.

The other side of criticism, the thing which brings us together, while criticism pushes us apart, is *appreciation*. I remember I started seeing this starkly when my relationship with my fiancée, Emma, began. I had come out of a long relationship which – for the last two years of it – included almost no appreciation. I had beaten myself up furiously as that relationship ended, noticing all the ways it was my fault. The power of Emma's appreciation as we got together changed me, and still does, each time she appreciates me.

So women, appreciate your men. You don't understand what a difference this will make to him. Before you want him to do something, appreciate him for what he has already done (he's so much more likely to do the thing you want if you appreciate him than if you don't, especially if you criticise him). Armstrong likens this appreciation to adding fuel to his fire. Whether it is for carrying shopping bags, for sorting something, for what he did with the children, for the work he does, or for just being there with you, appreciate him for who he is. It will bring you closer together and will allow him to be the man you want him to be, the man you fell in love with.

And men, appreciate your women. Appreciate them for what they do and do it as early as you can. Appreciate how nice she looks before you even leave the house, appreciate the work she has done, the things she has said, the things she has created in your home and in your work and in the world, as soon as you see them. Give her that gift, so she can relax with you, because before that, she may be in an early evolutionary space: on edge, asking 'does he like this?' And, under that question, 'will he still protect me?'

But more than that, appreciate her for who she is. Appreciate her for the way she lives her life. Because this will change her forever, supporting her to transform into an even more fulfilled, authentic version of herself.

We have such an opportunity to make our relationships transformational, to make them the route by which each of us grows, learns and develops into the people we – underneath – want to be. And, through the way we live, to give that gift to our children, to the people around us, to continue developing our amazing species.

The opportunity is in our appreciation of each other. For what we do, yes, but also the appreciation for who we are.

Chapter Twenty-Six

You Can't Make Someone Else Happy

Written on 18th September, 2019

Here's a thought I had recently: *what if it's not possible to make someone happy?* What if that just isn't possible. In the end, what if they have to make themselves happy?

Here's the difference I think it makes. First, we can remove from ourselves the blame that someone we love or care about isn't happy. It's not our fault. Wait, is that right? Maybe not quite; that might be too far. But at least, I think, we can say, 'it's not *all* our fault'.

And, if we don't have that blame, and if we can't *make* someone we love or care about happy, what can we do? Well, we can start, I think, by doing our absolute best not to make them *less* happy or *more* unhappy. That's a start, and that's better than nothing.

Maybe we can even do our best to make them a little happi*er*. A little *more* happy than they would be if we weren't here. That's better than nothing, too.

I think this distinction is important for three reasons: first, as I said, it relieves us of the pressure in our relationships that *it's all on us*. It's *never* all on you in a relationship with anyone. At the very least, it is on both of you.

And, it reminds us that it's not all on them, either. It's a relationship between two people (and I don't just mean a romantic relationship here; it could be any relationship). Both of you have contributed to what has been formed so far and both of you are creating the interaction now. At the very least, it's on both of you.

And, it gives us a place to go. We can do *something*. At the very least, at the times when people we care about are struggling, are unhappy, let's make sure we are doing everything we can to not make things worse. Or, to make things that tiny bit better than they would be without us.

The first step in that is what I write about in my forthcoming book, provisionally titled *The Power to Choose*. It's about making sure we are acting as the highest parts of ourselves – the wisest, most skilful, noblest parts of us – that we can at any time. Jordan Hall calls this being sovereign.

There are steps you need to take to do this. Here are some of the most important ones.

Make sure your physical energy is looked after: eat, sleep, drink water.

Do work on yourself to understand what patterns you are bringing to interactions with others, either from earlier parts of your life or from our evolutionary past.

Bring an assumption to your interactions with others: what if they are doing their best? And accept that all you can do, in this moment, is be the wisest and most skilful person you can be and give from that place.

You can't make someone happy. In the end, they have to do their own work on that. They have the power to choose and in those moments they have to use it. Life may make being *happy* now feel impossible for them. But it rarely makes it impossible to be *happier* or *less happy*. So take your responsibility seriously: don't be the person that makes them less happy, at least. Be skilful. And if you can, be someone who makes them just a tiny bit happier than they would have been without you, in whatever way you can. Be noble. Be wise.

Chapter Twenty-Seven

Holding Curiosity In All We Do

Written on 5th May, 2017

A few weeks ago, I was outside the Royal Festival Hall, standing on the terrace overlooking the River Thames, when I was approached by two police officers. I was due to meet a client and was on the terrace doing some exercises I do to gain focus before I coach someone. They raise my presence and bring up the quality of my work. There are two, one I designed and one I borrowed, and essentially they are both mindfulness exercises of a kind. For one I have my eyes closed and for the other I have my eyes open.

As I was part-way through the second exercise, the police officers came up to me and asked what I was up to. I explained. They were very friendly and, to my eyes and ears, seemed genuinely curious. They had seen me from below and said: 'I wonder what he's up to. If he's still up there when we get there, we'll ask him.' After I explained, one said: 'Maybe we could all do with more of that.' It was about 10 days after the terrorist attacks on Westminster Bridge and I was pleased to get an opportunity to speak to, be friendly to, and generally support the police officers who do so much amazing work around the country. And of course it's interacting with strangers, which as I'll discuss more in the next chapter is almost always strangely rewarding.

A few days later I discussed this with a couple of friends, one of whom is training to join the police. Both pretty much straight away said: 'They probably thought you were about to jump off or start a terrorist attack.'

As they said this, I instantly felt sad. I was disappointed at the idea that the two men weren't just curious about what was going on, and being friendly by interacting with a stranger. That they thought me to be a risk. And at first I thought: 'Wow, how cynical of my friends, to jump to that conclusion. They weren't there, they didn't see how calm, polite and friendly the officers were.'

And it is true that we can choose whether to be positive or negative, cynical or hopeful when we respond to things. Positive and hopeful gives us a more rewarding, enjoyable, wholehearted life, and helps others have this too. And so I will choose to believe for the most part that the police officers were asking just because they were curious.

But perhaps the greater lesson here is that the police officers were doing both. They were checking on the person standing quietly staring across the Thames, at a time of high security alert, as part of their job. And they were curious, calm, polite and friendly as they did it. And that is something we should all strive to be.

Chapter Twenty-Eight
Connecting With Strangers

Written on 12th January, 2017

Connecting with a stranger can be a magical moment.

Today, I ran for a train. The trains are crowded at Clapham Junction sometimes and there wasn't much space in the carriage. As I jogged towards the train, a blonde woman stepped back, ever so slightly, creating space for me, with a smile. We looked at each other. I said: 'Thank you.' And I felt better, and I knew what to write about.

Last night, I walked across Waterloo Bridge. There was a crowd of people looking over it down onto the south bank of the River Thames. There was a red carpet, for some kind of premier at the British Film Institute. Lots of people were there, journalists and photographers, shouting someone's name. I couldn't for the life of me work out who it was (it's hard to see who someone is from a very steep angle). In the end, I asked a couple of cheerful people next to me. They told me it was Ben Affleck and we joked about how he was wider than expected, or maybe it was just the angle, or maybe it was because he'd just played Batman. I felt better.

In some ways, these are small examples; in other ways, they are large. They are illustrative of what happens when we have longer conversations: at parties, at job interviews, with the person in the coffee shop. We are social animals, we need social interactions, and there's something magical about interactions with strangers. Here are three reasons for that:

1. The sense of possibility: who knows what might come of the conversation? Every relationship starts with two strangers speaking, who knows where this one may lead?

2. The sense of risk: when you put yourself out there, you don't know if someone will respond. It's brave to risk yourself. It's vulnerable. And courage like this is usually rewarded, inside or out.

3. The altruism: you don't know what's happening to another person that day. But whether it's good or bad, some unexpected kinship will always improve a day. And that feels good.

And here's the thing. Opportunities for these interactions are everywhere. My girlfriend, Emma, once managed to have conversations with something like four strangers in an eight-minute walk, some of whom were even in their cars, while she was walking. She came back beaming.

When we put our attention on things, we notice them. So put your attention on strangers. Notice them, and connect with them. See what happens.

Chapter Twenty-Nine
Don't Cheat The World of the Possibility of Partnerships

Written on 20th January, 2017

There is such a sense of possibility in partnerships. The right partnership, the right connection with another person or group of people, holds a power far greater than the sum of its individual members.

Just over a year ago, I met a fellow coach, Nicole Brigandi, at a Brené Brown talk. There started a partnership that has undoubtedly led to fascinating, creative and stretching work, which neither of us would have otherwise done. I've enjoyed that work so much more because of – and I wouldn't have managed it at all *except for* – that partnership. For us, this has involved a number of activities, ranging from our first work together, a session on team dynamics and objectives with an incredibly inspiring team of young leaders, to a video series on personal branding.

Partnerships hold so much potential. The potential is for practical support, when members of the partnership have other commitments, and for emotional support when the work gets hard. But it is the creative support that in many ways holds the real gold. A real partnership leads to the creation of things that just couldn't have existed with both people working on their own. That's the imperative behind partnerships.

Every time you turn down a partnership or don't pluck up the courage to start the one you want to start, you cheat the world of the outcomes – the creative outcomes – that could be the fruits of the connection between you and someone else.

And today, in this online, connection era, the possibilities are even greater. There is a world of partners at your fingertips.

Chapter Thirty

Love is a Transformational Practice

Written on 31st August, 2018

A practice changes you. Something that you do every day, week or month shifts things about you: sometimes the things you want to shift, and sometimes surprising things, too.

A practice of daily exercise will affect your physical health, but also other things. Perhaps something about your confidence. Perhaps the hormones you feel throughout the day and, through them, your very happiness. And, like any habit that you maintain, it affects your story about yourself: you are someone who can get up a bit earlier every day, you are someone who can follow through on their word and commitments. You are someone who recommits when things go wrong.

A writing practice has these multi-levelled effects, too. I set out on the writing practice of which this piece is part as a way to break my Resistance and grow my capacity to share with the world. That this is my 100th LinkedIn article, most of them as part of this practice, which has now lasted over two years, is a testament that it worked.

It has changed the way I write, too, which you might

expect. But it has also changed the way I think. And through that, it has changed the way I speak.

Seth Godin's words about his writing practice (daily, going back decades) have been an inspiration to me. He speaks about this in particular. Essentially, he says that he writes how he speaks. And, as Seth also says, if you write how you speak then you can't get writer's block because no one ever gets 'talker's block'. But there's even more to it than that: if you write how you think, then as your writing improves, so does the way you think. A writing practice is, in some ways, a practice in thinking. And if you write how you speak, it is also a practice in speaking. Something that changes the way you write, think, and speak. I'd call that a transformational practice.

I noticed this as I reflected on the speech I gave at my wedding a few weeks ago. I spoke in the speech about how I have been transformed by the love and appreciation I have received from my wife over the five years of our relationship. I spoke about this in terms of the way I speak publicly: I have moved from an actor, learning lines and delivering them well, to a more present, more confident, more comfortable speaker, telling stories from the heart and mind. And this transformation has come partly through a weekly practice of writing, and thinking, played out on LinkedIn. I have practised telling stories, forming sentences, making points, from the heart and mind, each week over two years. And

I saw some of the benefits of that as I spoke in front of a hundred of the most important people to me in the world.

But would I have got here – maintained the practice, stuck with it and all the other things I've done over the last five years – without five years of deep love and appreciation from my wife? I don't know; we can never know for sure. But what I do know is that I am transformed by that love, by that practice of love and appreciation that she has poured into me every day, every week. And I will never be the same, and I would never want to.

Love is a transformational practice, too.

So practise.

Part Three: CREATE ATTITUDES, MINDSETS AND MENTAL MODELS TO HELP YOU THRIVE

The break-up I wrote about in The 12-Minute Method section of this book has long felt like a watershed for me. It feels like it was the start of the journey to where I am now, although in reality it was just one more step on a much longer journey. But as I wrestled with the aftermath of that relationship and with my part in its end, I came to one of the most important realisations that a human can come to.

That is: how we think has an enormous impact on our lives. And, most importantly, we can change how we think. We can create attitudes, mindsets and mental models that are helpful to us, or ones that aren't.

In some ways, that's what all my writing is about. That's certainly the foundation of my work as a coach, and of many of the chapters in the 12-Minute Method series.

In particular, if we are thinking about creating the conditions for great work, then our attitudes, mindsets and mental models are where a huge part of the work will happen. How different would all our lives have been if we had always – as I wrote about in Chapter One – accepted our own mortality and simply acted, knowing we might never have the chance to be here again?

Simply by taking that attitude, which invites us not to hold ourselves back, my work would certainly have been greater more often. Indeed, as I said in the introduction, I count that piece among my absolute best, and it was written specifically with and about that mindset shift.

And so in Part Three you'll find a selection of shifts which might enable *you* to do more great work more often.

As with so many parts of this book, each of them could be the one for you for now. Each of them could allow you to see the world differently.

Coach and psychotherapist Mike Toller told me that every time he helps a client see things differently he has changed the world because he has changed how they see the world.

That's what's possible for you in this part: to change the world for yourself.

Let's see how it looks from the other side.

Chapter Thirty-One

Our Power to Create Our Own Reality

Written on 26th September, 2017

Here's a phrase I hadn't thought about much before yesterday: '*You don't want that.*'

It could be a father, say, looking after his son or daughter when she reaches for a snack that is too sweet or a DVD that it's too late to watch. Or a girlfriend to a boyfriend, about what he suggests doing or where he suggests going.

I heard Katie Hendricks talking about it on the Coaches Rising podcast. She was talking about it because some of the work she does as a coach is helping people get in touch with what they want. She says we aren't good at knowing that and part of that is because of phrases like '*you don't want that*'.

That phrase brings up an almost physical reaction in me, as I write it now. A rising feeling inside, which is getting ready to shout: '*YOU DON'T KNOW WHAT I WANT!*'

But most of the time that isn't what I have said during my life when people have said that, or something like it, to me. Mostly, people say it with such force, or confidence, or calm that I just believe them, until it's much later and

I'm wondering why I did or didn't do or say something in particular, something that I wanted to.

Of course that phrase is delivered with love, almost always. The person delivering it usually isn't thinking 'I want to suppress this person's ability to understand what they want,' or 'I want to impress my values on this person'. Mostly they are thinking – and really saying – 'I don't want that person to have or want that'. Sometimes that is because they are also thinking 'I don't think it's in the best interests of that person to have that thing.'

But language matters. If you're like me, with freedom and agency at the core of your values, then it's very important that we help people understand what they want. And it's very important we don't impose our views and values on others.

If you want an example of how important language is, try this. I learnt it from my friend Marie de Champchesnel at a coachingpartner seminar she facilitated.

Think of something at the moment that you feel like you *should* do. Or *must* do. Say it out loud a few times. I should go to the gym this evening. I must stop drinking in the week. I should write a blog post and post it on LinkedIn. Then replace the *should* or *must* with *could* or *choose to* or *want*, and repeat the sentence a few more times. I choose to go to the gym this evening. I could stop drinking during the week. I want to write a blog post and post it on LinkedIn. The different feeling you have is the feeling of agency, the feeling of creating your world. This is the feeling we can gift to others when we replace a phrase like 'you don't want that' with one like 'thanks for sharing what you want. I don't think that's the right thing for you now, and here's why...'

We have it in our power to create our own reality through the language we use and the thoughts we have. We also have it within our power to create the reality of others. So use the power wisely, and use it with care, and use it with love.

Chapter Thirty-Two
Listen for the Birdsong

Written on 29th June, 2018

Before almost every coaching session I do, I spend around 10 minutes on two practices. In different ways, they help take me into the presence I feel enables me to do my best work. One of them involves opening the nervous system to all the things that come to it, noticing them, then moving on and putting your attention back on your nervous system, ready to notice what comes next. This is an eyes-open practice and through it I have (via recommitting to the practice again and again, with MANY 'reps' of bringing my attention back when it has wandered) become more aware of my peripheral vision, of my senses, and of what I hear.

When I'm working from home, in the summer, I usually do these practices on our balcony, looking out over the view from our ninth-floor flat. It is in south-west London – Battersea – and the area is not particularly city-like, given its location relatively near the centre of a bustling metropolis. But when I tune into what my hearing picks up – when I notice the incoming sounds, allow them to arise, and then return to noticing what arises next – the sounds are mostly city. It is the children from the school across the road, the sound of construction not too far away, the traffic on the various main roads nearby. I see the sights of the city, too, the cranes, the helicopters, the cars and vans driving past. I see them, notice them, and return to seeing what I notice next.

I find one of the most beautiful and centring things to notice while doing this exercise is nature. The movements of the leaves on a tree in the breeze, the ripples on the river in the sun, birds flying in the sky. This connects me to something deeper.

One day, after living in this flat for perhaps 15 months, I noticed a thought during my centring exercise: it's sad that there are no *sounds* of nature in this place. Just the sounds of the city.

And then I heard it. Birdsong. And not just one bird, but several, from different directions.

I almost couldn't believe it. I was pretty sure I had *never* noticed birdsong in several months of standing on that balcony many times a week for five minutes at a time. I had always noticed the traffic noises, the banging. The children had been the most joyous sound I heard, as they regularly are.

But it touched me to hear the birdsong. And it made me think.

Next time I was practising, as I noticed a bird swoop by, I noticed another thought: I wonder if the birds are singing today. I hadn't noticed them up to that point. After

I wondered if they were singing, there was a van passing by. And then…there they were.

And it turns out they are *almost always* there. Only once since then when I have had that thought has it not been followed, shortly after, by noticing birdsong.

Our mind filters for things. It does its best and it keeps us sane. We couldn't cope with receiving all the information that is there in the world. Our brain filters for what it thinks is important. The part of the brain that does this is the reticular activating system. It's why you see many L plates when you are learning to drive, and lots of To Let signs when you are moving house. There aren't more at that time, but your reticular activating system is filtering for them.

The problem with this is it doesn't always get what is important right. And wherever you put your attention, it will think this is important and will show you more of it.

If you focus your thoughts on the idea that you live in a city, where there are buses and cars, construction and helicopters, and, yes, children, then you will hear those things. And you won't hear the birdsong.

Listen for the birdsong.

Chapter Thirty-Three
The Stories We Tell Ourselves Aren't Always True

Written on 17th August, 2016

There isn't usually much space on my train. It's often crammed with commuters, all silent, maybe plugged into some music or wisdom through their headphones. There's very little interaction; some passive-aggressive requests for people to move down, some exchanged smiles when someone does indeed move down. If something goes wrong – the train stops – there may be some shared grumbles.

Once, a man standing near me collapsed. Blacked out completely. And suddenly everyone moved. Two people next to him reacted fastest. They held him up, so he didn't crash to the floor and hurt himself. Suddenly there was concern all around. I offered some water and he didn't take it, but a woman next to me took the lead, took my water and made him drink. He was looked after by the seven people stood within a 90cm radius of him until we got to London Waterloo. And then, before I had even got off the train, someone was speaking to a member of station staff, who was already calling a first aider and moving towards the man. Even though the man said he was fine.

It's easy to think, especially in a city like London, that we aren't connected. That people are rude and grumpy. But actually, people do look out for each other, far more than you think. Those caring don't always show themselves, but they are there.

Today, my train is quite empty. I think the one just in front must have everyone on it. It's spacious. I could actually sit down if I wanted to, but I quite like standing and it's not far.

I'm not talking to anyone, but that doesn't mean I'm not connected. I'm writing this on my phone, and this short piece might connect me to 10 people, maybe 20, maybe more, maybe one. Probably at least to my mum.

It's easy to think that when someone is on their phone they are being insular, and they aren't out in the world, relating. But usually, when I'm on my phone, I'm interacting with more other people than most people in my grandparents' generation did at any one point in their whole life. Maybe I'm on my phone in the pub, with the football on, chatting to my friends across England about the match, and exchanging views with a Times journalist and some strangers about the evolution of the English language (as I did on Sunday).

It's easy to tell yourself stories about the people around you, but things like these remind me that they aren't always true.

Chapter Thirty-Four
Make Your Own Judgments

Written on 26ᵗʰ June, 2019

I had a strange conversation with a friend of mine a few weeks ago. I shared an idea I had learned from the work of clinical psychologist and author (and, let's not forget, internet sensation) Jordan Peterson. I think it was the way he described an ideology (something like: being able to predict everything someone believes based on knowing another thing they believe), but it could easily have been any number of his interesting ideas. My friend's reaction was stark:

'Jordan Peterson? I *hate* that guy.'

What made this especially interesting, as the conversation went on, was that it became apparent that my friend had no direct experience of Jordan Peterson. He hadn't read his book, he hadn't watched any videos; he hadn't even watched any of the (sometimes fairly viral) interviews Peterson has done. And yet the reaction was *strong*. There's a reason I put 'hate' in italics. That's how he said it.

This isn't the only conversation I've had like this, but it was the starkest, because this particular friend is someone I associate with being free-thinking, a scientist, interested in evidence and pursuing the truth. And yet here he was, jumping to a quite extreme conclusion, willing to speak forcefully about Jordan Peterson, without having interacted with *almost anything* about him.

I pushed my friend on this a little, remembering a tweet I saw in which someone said that she had made a decision years ago to only speak (or write) about people whose work she had read first hand. Only years later did she realise what a transformational practice this was. While I think in totality this is difficult and I don't quite hold this as tightly as she does, it is something I try to lean into. Before I jump to conclusions about someone or something, I try to think: 'Hold on a sec, Robbie. Can I watch or read or listen to something this person has said? Can I make my own judgment? What if they are being misunderstood here? What if I were to give them the benefit of the doubt?'

I was also empowered to push my friend by a brilliant response that Farrah Storr, then editor of Cosmopolitan UK, gave on Late Night Women's Hour. In response to another guest saying 'some people think of him [Peterson] as an arsehole', Storr said: 'A lot of people do. And to that I would say, he's got about 600 hours of videos on YouTube. Go through it all, look at it and then make an assessment.'

A few weeks after our conversation, my friend messaged me, saying he felt a little embarrassed about the strength of his reaction given he hadn't read Peterson's book. He sent me two articles which were – as far as he remembered – how he had formed his opinion about Peterson. I read them; they were (I thought) rather snipey articles from the New York Times and the Guardian. (I could almost have predicted what they said, of course, based on the ideologies of those publications, but I didn't: I waited until I had read them both, making my own judgments, before responding.) In these articles, they certainly weren't giving him the benefit of the doubt.

But why does this matter to me, to you or to us? Well, it matters because Jordan Peterson is an incredibly interesting thinker, deeply trying to help the world be a better place. In some ways, it makes complete sense that *I* would be interested in him. He has decades of clinical experience supporting people one-to-one and he is using that wisdom more broadly to try to help make the world a better place. Those two things are things I'm fascinated by and that I try to do in my own work.

But it's more than that. Jordan Peterson's work, and in particular his book, *12 Rules For Life*, is having an amazingly positive impact on many, many people. I had heard stories about this, but it was a few months ago when it really landed for me. I met a 21-year-old man who had been a student, and his life was getting out of control: drinking, drugs, who knows what else? He found Peterson's videos and took responsibility for his life: finding meaning, getting things in order, changing things, speaking the truth to try to change the university's culture at cost to himself. And there are literally thousands of other stories like this.

Jordan Peterson's work can be incredibly profound for people. He is certainly not 'evil', which some people seem to think. He is not 'alt right'. In my view, he is not worthy of hate. He is just a man struggling to do his best to make the world a better place.

The reason I'm writing this article (and to be completely honest I almost didn't, I almost felt unable to speak about it and there was serious Resistance) is because the work of Jordan Peterson has made a real difference to me and it has made a real difference to some of my clients, who have discovered it themselves or with whom I have shared some of his ideas.

The work of the press and certain parts of social media to paint Peterson as evil is quite 'of the modern age'. More on that, maybe, another time. This piece is simply me doing my bit to undo the kind of misinformation that people like my friend have absorbed. It is my encouragement to you: give him the benefit of the doubt. It might just change your life. Or the life of someone you know.

And wherever you can, make your own judgments.

* * *

Note: An interesting thing happened in the editing process for this book. The editor pointed out to me that a number of people who had previously been very engaged with Jordan Peterson's work have recently been raising concerns about his conduct, some seeing it as an abandonment of the principles that made his work so impactful for so many. A thoughtful piece on the subject is here:

https://rebelwisdom.substack.com/p/what-happened-to-jordan-peterson.

The interesting thing about this, of course, is that this chapter contains two clear messages: that Peterson's work has had a very positive impact on my life and the lives of many others: *don't believe everything you read.* And also, make your own judgments: *engage with someone's work before passing comment or settling into certainty.* So, what was I to do? My engagement with Peterson in the last couple of years has been limited to reading his latest book and listening to a couple of interviews. They gave me no concerns. But nudged by the editor and the article above I felt the need to engage further: I have to live the message of the piece and make my own judgment.

Watching a more recent Peterson video I found myself feeling something different to my past engagement with his work, seeing the concerns that others had raised. I considered a suggestion to remove the chapter, but it felt important to honour the impact of Peterson's work on me and on others *and* it felt important to maintain that second message, so important to me in making great work in the complexity of the world: make your own judgments. Mine is that what I wrote in this chapter – snapshot in time as it is – still warrants including in this book based on everything I know now. But more importantly, you need to make your own judgments: on Jordan Peterson, on me, on others. Take the good and the bad, the smooth and the rough. Listen, and see whether you think someone has something important to say. And remember that mostly, people are more complex and nuanced than we assume.

This has prompted much thinking from me about what it takes to navigate the possibility of the information age without falling into its traps: all the mindsets, balances and decisions we make about who to listen to and when. What are we to do with imperfect humans who say one thing in one place and another in another? What if someone says something that inspires us in one place and something that disgusts us in another? All people change: what are we to do about that? When have we done *enough* engaging with someone's work to make a judgment? Those questions are too long to attempt to answer even in this very long note, but they're important to consider.

Chapter Thirty-Five
What Are You Committing To?

Written on 31st August, 2017

We make commitments all the time. Sometimes we break them. Sometimes after days, sometimes weeks, sometimes years.

Sometimes breaking our commitments makes no difference to anyone else. Sometimes it inconveniences them. Sometimes it breaks their hearts.

And sometimes we hold to those commitments to the ends of the earth. Sometimes wisely, sometimes blindly.

The power of a commitment is that it holds you when you doubt. The strength of them is often decided by the depth of the commitment and the place you are making it from.

Sometimes this commitment is to ourselves. Sometimes to our Future Self, and we are grateful to our Past Self for the commitments he held to. Sometimes the commitment is to our Past Self, to show her that we have learned from the trials, tribulations and joys that she experienced. Sometimes it is a commitment made by our Past Self, which we are holding to in order to honour him.

And sometimes our commitment is to someone else. To a lover, a parent or a child, alive or dead. To a leader or a follower, current, past, or future. And, sometimes, our commitment is to something bigger. To the depths of our soul, which is calling us. To the universe, which is asking us.

So ask yourself, which commitments am I holding to? And which am I not? To who or what did I make this commitment?

Because sometimes we get confused. Sometimes we hold to commitments from the past, commitments never asked of us. Or commitments to someone, within us or out there, who we now know was wrong.

Sometimes our commitment to safety, to comfort, to adventure, to rebellion, takes us somewhere. And in that place we lose sight of the commitments. The promises we made ourselves, or others. Sometimes we find ourselves believing those commitments are a real part of ourselves. And sometimes safety, comfort, adventure and rebellion aren't what we need.

And here. Here is the question. What is the deepest commitment you are making? Looking inside. What is your deepest self asking of you? What is life asking of you? And what, here, are you willing to commit to?

You don't have to tell anyone. You might not change anything, but the power is in the question. Because then, then you can decide. Then you can look at the commitments you are breaking, leaving to drift, and you can see that you have chosen these. You have chosen another commitment over this one. And that is human. That is the challenge of our life: to change our commitments, with clarity and conscience, with courage and with love. With the knowledge that we are not perfect and sometimes we need to shift the commitments we have. With forgiveness, for ourselves, and for others.

With integrity, for this is who I am. And it is not who I was before. And perhaps something is calling me. Something deeper. Something bigger.

What is calling *you*?

Chapter Thirty-Six
It's Good To Own Your Gifts

Written on 22nd February, 2019

I've noticed a thing I do well. It's about creating stories. Stories that make sense to people. Connecting dots for them, drawing those dots together into something the person is happy to share, to help them get what they want.

[Hint: the way to do this is by telling the truth, more, with skill.]

Sometimes this is to help a client introduce themselves. A client I spoke to last week was asking how they can talk about coaching. She joked: 'I've worked in teaching people communication for 10 years and I can't communicate this.'

'That's it,' I said. 'When someone asks you what you do, you say: "Well, it's funny: I've been training people in communication for 10 years, but the work I do is hard to explain, is hard to communicate even for me because this thing coaching, it's powerful, and it's magical, and it's hard to describe."'

Another client came across the video series I created with my friend Nicole Brigandi about mastering your personal brand. She was answering the questions we pose in one of those videos, and suddenly emerging from her was a newfound confidence as she realised her previous experience suddenly sounded powerful when she spoke about it in certain ways. Suddenly she didn't feel like such a beginner in her new business any more. Because she wasn't. Because she'd been doing the work for 30 years, but she hadn't realised it until that moment.

Often, I'll coach people on the difficult conversations they want to have with their boss, or their partner, or a colleague. They'll tell me about it, articulating beautifully the challenges they face, and often showing deep understanding and compassion for the other person. And then they'll say: 'How do I tell them this?'

And often I find myself being the voice in their life, asking: 'What would happen if you told the truth, like you've just told it to me?'

But this isn't just about telling the truth. This is about one of the deepest and most important communication skills, storytelling. 'But wait,' people sometimes ask, as I sometimes suggest sharing (only) part of what is happening in their life, truthfully, with their boss, perhaps not mentioning everything. 'Isn't this dishonest or inauthentic?'

And the answer is, 'that depends'. But we never tell the full truth. We never tell everything. There is always storytelling happening. We don't share every thought with even our closest loved ones. We can't, because we think faster than we speak, and we aren't with them all the time. It is literally impossible to tell everything. We are always sharing only a select view of what we have seen in the world.

And so why not choose what we share with more skill?

That's one of the gifts that I've noticed I have, this week in particular. I joy in doing it, in finding the story people can tell for themselves or, more usually, to share with the world about what they feel in themselves. But the gift isn't just any story; it's a story that is coherent, that makes sense to them, and will make sense to the world. An honest reason to be doing what they are doing.

And it got me thinking, where did this thing that I do, that I love to do, come from?

I think it started early. One of the great gifts my parents gave me was to help me see things from other people's perspectives. Almost all parents do this ('How do you think Graham felt when you hit him on the head with your plastic train?'), but mine, I think, had a particular proficiency, bringing with them skills of counselling and psychotherapy as well as a deep curiosity about how the world, and people, work.

Then I honed that skill: I spent hours (sometimes with my brother, sometimes alone) playing elaborate games with action figures, sometimes superheroes, sometimes Action Force, sometimes other things: ThunderCats, He-Man, Captain Planet. These were deep and intricate games with characters and depth. Slipping into the people, their relationships, their adventures. These stories were real and they were coherent. Sometimes they lasted days at a time.

Then I honed it further. Aged 11, I started acting: in a school play as a First World War soldier, singing carols across the trenches at Christmas. And I spent the next 15 years spending hundreds if not thousands of hours doing this, playing other people, getting into their characters. I remember, aged 15, on a course with the National Youth Theatre, hating the part I had...until I found the way to understand the person, to make his story coherent. Then it made sense and I found joy in it. I remember this moment repeating again and again over the years as I realised how much I enjoyed finding that story, the one that made sense, even for characters that were unsympathetic, and even for those who were evil.

Then I honed it further. I have applied for a lot of jobs in my life. I imagine 30 or more. I have re-purposed myself as someone who people should employ in finance, in arts leadership, in HR, in learning and development, as a coach. And within each of those categories I have strived to find the way to make my story, my CV, make sense and be coherent so that *of course* they could hire me for this job. Sometimes it has worked, sometimes it hasn't, but the stories I have told have (mostly) been good.

And now I do it for my clients, who don't know how to talk about themselves, or don't know how to reach out to their own clients in a way that feels genuine and not icky, or don't know how to contact someone who inspires them to ask them for mentorship, or don't know how to speak to their boss about something that is troubling them.

And it feels like a gift, for me and for them, every time I can complete that pattern, every time I can join the dots for them, every time I can find the truth that resonates in this moment.

So here we are. I have told a story. Does it make sense? Is it coherent? Does it resonate in this moment?

What are your gifts and where did they come from? It feels important that you own them.

Chapter Thirty-Seven

Where Our Greatest Strengths and Our Greatest Struggles Intersect

Written on 20th June, 2018

I was at an event in April. I was in a small group speaking about what edge I wanted to lean into that weekend (it was a coaching event, where that is the kind of thing you get asked). For me, it was about worrying less about what people think.

Simon Crowe, leading the group, then shared something. He said: 'The thing about worrying about what people think is: to worry about it, you have to be really good at understanding what other people think.'

You see, the thing about the things we struggle with is that they are often deeply connected to the things we do really well.

My work is about spending time with people, helping them really understand what is going on in their life. A lot of it is about understanding what they think. I wouldn't be as good a coach without having this gift.

And the funny thing is that, as Simon said, it means I am incredibly good at imagining what people may be thinking.

I am also good at examining things intellectually. I may have always had this, but I honed it in three years at university studying mathematics. That brings an intellectual rigor to the way I solve problems. Looking at things from different angles, trying on for size different ways of solving problems.

This is something else my clients value in my work.

But when you add those together, they hold me back: from writing things, from saying things, from trying things. I am good at understanding what people might be thinking, and at examining what they might be thinking from lots of different angles. And that leads me to worry about what other people think, which leads me to hold back in all sorts of ways from a fear of the possible negative reaction they might have (which I happen to be very good at imagining).

Two of my greatest strengths add up to one of the things I have struggled with for many years.

Of course it didn't start that way. At some point in my life – probably when I went to school, starting formal education aged eight after being educated at home up to that point – it was really important to understand what people thought. I didn't understand the rules and people at school often thought really differently to how my family did. By learning to understand, I could fit in. I could be safe.

And that safety mechanism developed into something I could do really well, and many years later I found a profession, coaching, which made full use of this gift. Seeing perspectives, examining problems.

So now the challenge becomes, how do I use the strengths when they help, but let them go when they hold me back? That is the challenge.

But not just for me: for you, too.

Chapter Thirty-Eight

We Are the Sum of Our Experiences

Written on 17th March, 2017

This weekend I am returning to the beautiful corner of northern England where I grew up. I know what it'll be like, the feeling of seeing the familiar train stations, and then faces, and then stepping back into the old Yorkshire house where I grew up. At some point in my stay, probably looking out across the valley of green fields to the moors in the distance, surrounded by familiar smells and sounds, and people, I'll sigh. There will be a release. *Home.*

I'll also be seeing some of my oldest friends. This is a different experience to any other group I have. I've known these people for more than a decade, two decades in some cases. We'll do those things that groups of men have done together across millennia. We'll compete with each other; we'll talk about other men competing with each other. We'll use nicknames that are as old as our friendships. And we'll laugh, a lot. These people are home, too.

We are the sum of our experiences. And the experiences of our ancestors, over thousands of years. They are a part of us. And being in the presence of those things that form a particularly big part of us: the people, the places, the singers, the songs and the rest, of course. Being in the presence of those things is a relief. It is affirming. It is strengthening. It is joyful. Because it is who we are.

Take some time today. Remember those people, those places, those singers and songs. Take a moment to acknowledge how they formed you, for better and for worse. Because you can't take them back. You can't do away with them. That doesn't mean they rule you, or there won't be other things that match them for significance across the length of your life. But let them in a little, today. Let yourself in. These things. They are who you are.

Chapter Thirty-Nine

Your Failures Are Part of the Journey

Written on 7th May, 2019

A couple of weeks ago I was running a workshop at the University of Edinburgh, with my friend Jo Hunter and her company, 64 Million Artists, for a group of leading researchers who are experts in their fields. As part of the workshop, two senior leaders further on in their journey than the participants on the programme came to talk about their leadership journeys and one of them did something I had never seen before.

She had spent most of her short talk speaking about the challenges of her job – a role she loved. But before she finished, she listed out all the jobs she had applied for while in her previous role. There were eight jobs on the list, including some she hadn't even been shortlisted for, and she spoke about the challenges of this. The eighth job on the list was the one she was in: one she loved; one she had finally been successful with.

Wow, what a powerful lesson. That evening, over dinner, one of the researchers on the programme shared how he does a similar thing with colleagues just starting out in academia: sharing lists of all the grants he *hasn't* got, all the papers that *haven't* been published.

Thankfully, the explosion of tech companies has, in business at least, shown us the value of being open to failure. But personally, it is still so rare to see someone list, in the cold light of day, the times they haven't made the cut.

On my way to the station today, knowing I would be writing this piece, I opened a spreadsheet I keep of all the coaching I have done since I first started training with The Coaching School in June 2015. The bottom half contains all the people I have been paid to coach. The top half, though, contains a list of all the people I have gifted coaching to without being paid a penny.

There are 141 names on that top half of the spreadsheet. These are people I have coached, giving my absolute best to, but they have not become clients. I have spent a total of 288 hours coaching those people, not one of whom has ever paid me to coach.

They don't feel so much like failures right now, partly because I have learnt the power of chasing 'No', and partly because I have currently got my equivalent of the leader from the University of Edinburgh's ideal job. I've got the good ending: a group of clients I am inspired to work with.

But on that list of 141 people are also my struggles and mistakes; people who could have been among the most inspiring clients I could ever hope to work with.

Now, I'm lucky in this case. Because of the way I work, they *were* among the most inspiring clients I could ever hope to work with. They are part of my journey now, just as I am part of theirs.

But make a list of your failures. The relationships that didn't work out. The chances missed. The jobs you didn't get. The clients who said no. Share them (share them with me if you want to). Raise a glass to them.

They're part of who you are. You wouldn't be you without them.

Chapter Forty
Yes, and

Written on 24th October, 2017

One of the reasons that I enjoy listening to the Tim Ferriss show is some overlap of shared worldview with the host. There are many ways that this seems to show up, but curiosity about people and a general sense of optimism and wonder about humans and the world are perhaps the clearest parts of it.

Today I found Tim's guest, Richard Branson, leaving me feeling a little contraction around some of his views. They didn't seem to add up with mine – or with many of Tim's guests' – in a few areas.

And, as has been my practice for a number of years, upon feeling contraction I got curious (because, as Guy Sengstock once said, the opposite of contraction isn't openness, it's curiosity). And here's what I found: as well as my belief in our ability to interpret our reality in so many different ways, to decide it, to make it up, to choose our own adventure, I believe there is a deeper truth, and it is worth seeking. This leads me to triggers and disagreements and discomfort when I see someone missing what I see as an important, fundamental detail.

So when Branson says all wars can be avoided, essentially through negotiation, I want to get him in a room and ask him how you negotiate with someone who kills little girls at a pop concert because they are infidels. There are two parts of that: I want to point out that he may not have seen all of it, but I also want to know the answer. Richard Branson is an arch-deal maker. *How would he make the deal with ISIS?* Then, he might learn and I might learn. And the truth comes closer for both of us.

At the start of that fictional conversation there is disagreement, and I worry. I worry that it may sound like I don't want an end to war. But I do. It's just that I'm not sure Richard has got it quite right.

I find myself in similar conversations with people in real life. My aunt, for instance, may think I believe that it's no problem if tigers become extinct, because I pointed out to her that headlines are rarely written about the species of animals that are appearing in the world. An old friend may think I believe there is no space for supporting others through a welfare state, or no point in the regulation of business, because I spoke about the power of the free market to change the word.

And it makes me wary. It makes me wary of sharing those views. This week, in the face of the Me Too hashtag on Facebook, I felt a call to speak to the men out there, like me, who have always tried to live an honest, good life, but have undoubtedly done things – things they regret – that may have spawned a Me Too moment, posted on Facebook or not. But – and I think some of this is real, although some may just be my fear – expressing a nuanced view is often seen and responded to, particularly online, as a denial. As a 'No, But'. In fact, it's meant as a 'Yes, And'.

And there is a choice in that moment, for each of us as we read or hear the view of someone we disagree with. We *can* choose our own reality here. We can see these comments by people we disagree with as a 'No, But'. As confrontation. As false. As something that is never true and never will be. Or we can see it as a 'Yes, And'. Somewhere in the words someone is speaking to you is a truth. A truth of theirs. A truth of ours.

Yes, we could negotiate more with people before fighting them. And, sometimes people can't be reasoned with.

Yes, tigers going extinct would be an enormous tragedy. And we can enjoy the wonder of a new species of cricket evolving on a Hawaiian island.

Yes, we need to regulate business and look after the most vulnerable people. And, we need to notice what the amazing rise of the free-market economy has done to improve the lives of billions by almost any measure.

Yes, we need to care for, and speak for, and listen to, and empower women who have been through terrible, terrible experiences. And, we need to notice those who are regretting their actions, and help them to know that although they *did* bad, it is not that they *are* bad.

This is the truth as I see it. What do you see?

Chapter Forty-One
Feeling Change in the Air

Written on 20th June, 2017

It's hot in London at the moment. Almost as hot as it gets in the UK. When I left my flat this morning, though, I sensed a change in the air. 'The weather,' I thought, 'is changing.' Now as it turns out, I was wrong. I'm now on the train, sweating in the stifling heat with the sun beating down on the un-air-conditioned train.

But something struck me about that. There's a sense of relief in the heat ending. Some of that is because I don't sleep well when it's warm and it would be nice to go somewhere without sweating. But I love the sun, really, so the idea of a return to grey London being grey London being a relief struck me as strange. The feeling was familiar, though. It's the same feeling I get when I realise I'm getting better after a cold. And it's very similar to the feeling that the week is coming to an end and the weekend is coming. I've equated that weekend feeling, the Friday feeling, with freedom in the past. But I now suspect there's another element at play. Change.

Because that's what I'm feeling when I realise the weather is about to break and that's what I'm feeling when I sense my cold is passing. And that the working week is coming to an end.

Change is a powerful thing for humans. There's something undeniably exciting about it and I think part of this is because there's a strong resistance in most people to the idea of being trapped. To things being *exactly like this* forever. There's a fear of it. What if it is this hot *forever*? What if I *never* get better?

And that's why the sense that things are changing, right in front of us, gives that flicker of excitement. It is the knowledge that things will be different and that's exciting. An excitement not always without fear, of course, but it is *something new*. And in the relief from fear of being trapped is the beckoning of control. With control comes freedom.

And change always comes. Remember that. Nothing is the same forever. Right here, right now, something is changing. Listen for it and maybe you can feel the freedom.

It's very warm on my train, but I love the sun. I'm glad it's here. But when that next drop of rain comes, I will joy in the rush of excitement. Things change.

Chapter Forty-Two
Wonderful is Just a Moment Away

Written on 9ᵗʰ November, 2018

A couple of months ago, I was in a conversation with two fellow coaches. We were discussing coaching, and a phenomenon that most coaches will recognise: that sometimes sessions feel really hard. Change and transformation are not always linear and my experience has been that often around 50 to 75 per cent of the way through a coaching engagement, it will start to feel really hard. The 'easy', reflective bit is done, and the exciting external results haven't all materialised yet. It feels like no progress has been made.

My old coach Rich Litvin sometimes points out that if you're on an exponential curve and everything feels flat, you don't know if you are right next to where everything starts to fly upwards at hyper speed. But you could be.[1] And that's my experience in coaching: often following some of the most difficult, hardest conversations – the conversations when we are most convinced we are on the flat with no change in sight – something unlocks, and there come the extraordinary results.

Sometimes, wonderful is just a conversation away.

That's what I said to my colleagues, and one of them, Nina O'Farrell, wrote it down and said: 'I'm going to remember that. It's the kind of thing you should get put up on your wall, next to whatever other inspirational quotes you have.'

This week, I learnt something more. I had a conversation with a client. It was hard. We could both feel it. We didn't have the flow or the energy of our previous conversations. We played some more. It was still hard.

And then…something changed. I won't speak about what, because that is private and confidential, but what I will say is that after a slow, staccato first half of the conversation, the second half of the conversation is one I think I will remember forever. Tears pricked my eyes more than once, and almost slipped down my cheeks. I don't know what results will happen for the client, but I could feel the power of the conversation.

And I realised that, if we want it, wonderful is closer than a conversation away. Wonderful is just a moment away.

Not perfect, not happy, but wonderful. Full of wonder. *That* is just a moment away.

That's hard to remember in our lives; our busy, tricky lives. It's hard to find that thing that might shift and it's hard to shift it. Sometimes, we *are* on the flat part of the exponential curve, very near the X axis, and what transformation will take is slow and steady action and thought. But sometimes, sometimes we are way to the right on the X axis. It still feels flat, but we are *right next to* the moment when everything changes.

And here's what I think. Life isn't even as linear as an exponential curve. Because if we live life as though we are on the flat, a long way from when our change curve takes off, we stay there. But if we live life as if we are *right next to* the moment when everything changes, then things open up. Things spread out. Things change.

That's what happens when we live life from a place where wonderful is just a moment away.

Notes

1. If you don't know what an exponential curve looks like, go to **www.robbieswale.com/wonderful** to see what I'm talking about.

Chapter Forty-Three

Don't Miss the Moments as They Are *Coming*

Written on 13th May, 2019

The chances in our life to watch someone's dreams coming true are so rare. We had one last week. I was on a train, and missed it live, but later I watched it back as a reporter played the Brazilian commentary on Tottenham Hotspur's remarkable win away at Ajax back to Spurs' Brazilian forward Lucas Moura.

The translation of the commentary is amazing. They shout 'It had to be you, Lucas!' and 'It's from the heart!' as Lucas scores a goal that took Spurs through and sent Ajax out with what could have been the last kick of the game. I was able to watch a video of Lucas seeing the commentary, just minutes after the final whistle, and watching himself – with brilliant technical skill – receive Dele Alli's flick and execute a finish so quickly that the goalkeeper could barely move. The emotion in him was palpable; you don't need a translation to feel the energy of the moment, to feel for this man. You don't even need to know his story, but I'll tell it anyway: a promising forward who struggled to get a place in the team at Paris Saint-Germain and moved to Tottenham 18 months ago, only playing because of Harry

Kane's injury, and he scored not once, not twice, but three times as Spurs came back from 3-0 down on aggregate, away from home, to reach the Champions League final for the first time. But what he says as he watches it, wiping tears away from his eyes, is that he has been dreaming of winning the Champions League since he was a little boy. And now he is playing in the final. And he scored the goals that took his team there, each one requiring not only skill but nerve, courage and – yes – heart.

It reminded me, as I watched it back this morning, of Wayne Rooney breaking the England goalscoring record. Even though some of the ability that had made Rooney such an explosive player in the first half of his career had left him, and even though he may – as he broke the record – have been holding the England team back, seeing that moment as he scored his 50th goal for England, breaking Bobby Charlton's decades-old record of 49 goals, I felt the emotion of it. And his team-mates knew, too, running from the other end of the field to congratulate him. This wasn't just any goal. It was the dreams of a little boy from Liverpool fulfilled before our eyes.

He used to have those dreams, I don't doubt, as he played wherever he played when he was little. He, like I, like so many children, knew about Charlton's 49 goals and Lineker's 48, and probably commented to himself – like I did – on the fictional World Cups played in his imagination on a front lawn or a street corner. And there, as he scored the penalty, that dream was fulfilled.

It is what makes the Olympics special: these rare occasions, just once every four years, which someone has been working towards potentially their whole life. And we get to see those moments.

And as I sit here this morning, reflecting, I wonder about Lucas Moura and about his manager, Mauricio Pochettino, who also struggled to hold back the tears. Because they haven't won the Champions League yet. They won't be favourites in the final against Liverpool. I wonder if this will be the height of it, the height of the emotion. It was from the psychologist Jordan Peterson that I learnt the idea that fulfilment comes not from achieving our goals, but from *seeing our progress towards them*. I've felt this to be true in my life, and I wonder if that is one of the reasons that this moment for Lucas, and for Pochettino, is so special. They are still on their journey towards their dreams.

The dreams are important. They are what guide us in our lives, if we dare to dream. And the progress is important: noticing the moments, as Lucas did on Wednesday, when we are achieving monumental things in pursuit of our dreams.

Not all of us dream of fame and fortune, not all of us have (or should that be 'score'!) such public goals. That moment of dreams coming true can show up in the most surprising – and expected – of places: the hospital as a child is born, the office as an email is sent, the hilltop as the mountain is climbed, the shop as a product is sold.

But notice, for a moment, the language that I – unthinkingly – used at the start of this article. The chances in our life to watch someone's dreams *coming* true. An active word, an emergent word.

Don't miss the moments as they are *coming*.

Chapter Forty-Four
The Undertaker's Eyes

Written on 5th June, 2019

I went to my grandmother's funeral a few weeks ago. There were many ways, of course, that the day was memorable, not least the sense of the end of an era: a bridge to more distant relatives had left the world.

But as I got on my train back from Darlington to London, one of the things that most stuck in my mind was the experience of meeting and shaking the hand of the undertaker who had brought grandma's body from Reeth, in the Yorkshire Dales, to the crematorium for the funeral.

There was something about him as he shook my hand before and after the ceremony. Something about the way that he spoke to me. Something about his eyes.

I spoke to my mum and dad about it afterwards, in the bar of the hotel where we had held the wake, as the guests left until it was just my parents, my sister and me. They knew what I was talking about and said their experience with the other undertaker, the one in the village who took care of the first part of the process, was the same. Memorable. With a quality to it not easy to define.

These men had both, as we understood it, become undertakers as part of the family business. They had been doing it since they were maybe 15 years old.

As I reflected on this, I thought of the impact that thinking about death has had on me, and on my clients. And then I thought about the experience of dealing with death every week, from the age of 15 onwards. Being part of these impossibly difficult moments for people, these moments of loss, and grief, and anger, and frustration, and love. And humanity, deep humanity. Every week.

Most of us ignore the prospect of death (we see it as a certainty for everyone else, but somehow never for ourselves). Fred Kofman says that CEOs who have had near-death experiences perform better as leaders, and no wonder. Facing your death unavoidably puts life into a different perspective, and must free you to behave so much more in line with your values, seeing the world as it is, not as you wish it was. And so must facing death every day of your adult life, I imagine.

I know what it's like to sit with someone when they are facing tragedy in their life, from my friends, my family and my clients. Along with the sadness and empathy, it is enriching and enlivening and – of course – deeply emotional. The presence of the undertaker, the love in his eyes and his heart, still feels almost tangible to me weeks later.

And what a life's work it is to do that every week, for your whole life. It makes me wonder, given the power that considering our own death has for any normal person, what life is like as an undertaker. And it makes me wonder what life would be like if we all had the presence and depth that this man from Yorkshire had as he shook my hand in a Darlington crematorium.

I think we would be free from so much of the angst – my brother recently called it 'the madness' – that seems to flood the modern world. I think each of us would be able to be what Jordan Hall calls 'sovereign' more often, far more often.

And I think from there we would be able to create so much more from this world, individually and as a race. So I wish you a sense of your own mortality. It doesn't sound like something you would want, but I think it might be best for all of us if we had it.

Chapter Forty-Five

It's Time to Let the Wisdom Emerge

Written on 28th November, 2017

This series of pieces began as a practice, to break through my Resistance and allow myself to grow. As a practice to help me share myself, freely, with the world. It came from a place of discomfort: the contraction and fear of sharing. And it came from a place of courage: a growing understanding that only by facing our greatest resistance and fear can we really grow into the people we have the potential to be. It came from a place of acceptance: if, as Steven Pressfield says, the more important an action is to our soul's evolution the greater the Resistance we will feel, then we can use it as a compass, to find our way to a better place, a deeper place, a more fulfilled place. A more full-souled place. If that is true, we need to accept that Resistance is there and get on with making art anyway.

Sometimes the pieces started with a thought, brewing on my walk to the train. Sometimes they started with an interaction, a shared smile with a stranger, for example, suddenly opening up an idea. What I didn't know when they started, in August last year, was that they were really a practice in creating from the Through Me place. In allowing what emerges to emerge through me and out into the world. Sometimes it didn't feel much like that: sometimes it was By Me creation, which is wonderful too: something I had thought about and formed on the walk to the train or in the shower. Sometimes it was even To Me writing, to a certain extent: creating something from the place I was at that time, victim of the struggles and the thoughts rattling around in my head. But even in those To Me and By Me moments, it was and is a Through Me practice. Because I don't know where this piece is going to end today, and even if I did I wouldn't know how it would get there. Because there's no time to waste in 12 minutes, you just have to write and see what happens.

I wrote a longer piece from a Through Me space in August this year, as that became the end I sought rather than an accident of creation. I read it back the other day and it is powerful. And it is strange. I don't really remember writing it. Some of it doesn't really sound like me. It sounds like someone or something else. I'm going to share it this week. Through Me is really what happens when you get Resistance – which is primarily a battle fought in the head – out of the way. When you get fear out of the way, at least a little. When you bypass your thoughts and release the inner wisdom in you. You do it, sometimes, in conversation. You do it, sometimes, with your art. I do it, sometimes, in my coaching. If you're a coach, you probably do, too.

Nature will take you there, out of your head and thoughts. Music will take you there, too. Or at least it will for many of you. Sometimes reading will, sometimes theatre will. I find those a little less good at it. Playing the guitar takes me out of my head. Standing in our spare room in our flat in London, when no one else is home, singing and playing, allowing the sound of some song learnt a decade or more ago to flow out. I don't have to think about the chords to *Foxy's Folk Faced* any more. The beauty and the poetry just come out of me. It's mostly not mine. It's mostly Simon Fowler's. But there's a flavour of me. Especially now, after 15 years of playing it. And that, really, is what it is like to write these pieces, sometimes. It is what it was like to write the longer piece. Did it really come from me? Does art really emerge from 'me', the me that I think of? Or did it come from somewhere else?

I remember this feeling from acting, too. My best acting came from releasing what I was supposed to do. From knowing it, embodying it, doing almost all of it, *and* dancing and living in the moment, as the character. That's where the magic happened.

I notice it in my coaching, these days, more and more as I practise. I'm not thinking about what to do (most of the time), I'm just seeing what emerges. And that's where the magic happens.

There are wonderful places for tactics and strategies. I love the way the rational mind has created wonders the likes of which our grandmothers and great uncles could never have imagined. But I'm curious about what comes next, now, as we release that. As we lean into our deeper wisdom. As we include our emotions and our body intelligence in the magic of what we can create. As we listen for something bigger and something deeper.

What will come next?

Afterword

Written on 19th July, 2022

And then here we are again.

The end of the book.

One of my most prevalent thoughts in writing this series, as I turned what I created, 12 minutes at a time, into a series of books, has been 'I haven't done enough.'

I haven't done enough to help people start.

I haven't done enough to help people keep going.

I've haven't done enough. There's more I could have said.

That feels more true with this book, probably, than with either of the previous two. It's a grand promise: to help you create the conditions for great work. And I can't know if I'll help you with that.

If you find some of the great thinkers in the field and read their work on this, you can certainly find things that look more like a formula for great work. Ones you can use.

I can't be sure that what's here will help you create the conditions for great work. That is the sad truth for me, and the kind of thought that flies into my mind late at night. So what can I be sure of?

I can be sure that no great work is created unless you start. So make sure you start.

I can be sure that great work that could otherwise have been created has not been created because people gave up on something that they deep down didn't want to give up on. So keep going.

And I can be sure that the ideas, thoughts, habits, mindsets, reflections and actions in this book have helped me live a happier and more fulfilled life.

And living a happier, more fulfilled life has given me the mental, emotional and spiritual space to do better work.

As I have been able, through wrestling with all the things I've outlined in this book, to be more me, I have been able to do more work. And more of that work has been what I would call 'great'.

Not, perhaps, 'great' in the way that some people would think. I don't have millions of followers or millions of pounds.

No politicians or elite sportspeople or CEOs of world-famous companies know my name (as far as I know).

But that's not necessarily what greatness is about.

I know what the feeling of greatness is like for me. The feeling of what Gay Hendricks might call my Zone of Genius.

I know the feeling of being in that place, of having got out of my own way enough to be in flow as I coach, or speak, or write, or create.

I know that sometimes, when I have created the conditions to do great work, the absolute best work I could have done in that moment has emerged.

Well, maybe I don't *know* that. I don't know that I couldn't have done better. But I know that I've done better this time than I would have done in the past.

And, really, that's all we can hope for. Are we creating better work today than we did yesterday? Than we did last year?

Are we doing the things that will take us there? That will take us towards our potential, towards our unique genius, towards that magical work that we might do. That *only* we can do.

If we're doing our best to do that, and doing our best to not make things worse as we do it, then we can feel confident that we are making our contribution to tilt the world we all live in together towards heaven and away from hell.

In that last paragraph is something important that has emerged for me in the last year or so.

This work – helping people with their creative projects, their creative battles – is, for me, about creating the kingdom of heaven on earth.

I'm not religious, but if we're thinking about purpose, purpose that really matters, something that connects to the deepest parts of ourselves and others, then sometimes we need that kind of grand, mythopoetic language.

There are two ways that this work tilts the world towards heaven.

The first is that it feels like hell when we have something we want to create and we aren't creating it. The unsung song, the unwritten book, the unasked-out person, the unstarted business. Hell. And I know that feeling.

If you do this work, the work that really matters to you, you will tilt the world towards heaven, because you will make your creative hell dissipate. It will feel completely different once you have taken the steps of courage to start, to keep going, to create the conditions for greatness to emerge and then to share your work.

The second way that this work tilts the world towards heaven is that I have never spoken to anyone about their creative dreams and found it to be something selfish, something without broader value. Always, it has at least in part been about creating something that helps the world be more good, true or beautiful. And so as we all do this work, the work that really matters to us, we are tilting the world towards heaven.

That, then, is what this book is about.

It is about how to help you do that work, the work that really matters to you.

How to get out of your own way.

How to tilt your life away from hell and towards heaven.

How to do great work, that will help all of us live better lives, more happy, more fulfilled.

Please – do that work.

Help Spread the Word

I believe that the world is a better place when people are creating things; when people move out of the hell of procrastination and make things that make a difference.

If you agree with me, or if this book has helped you, please help someone else start when they're stuck by doing one of two things:

1. Review this book on Amazon

It really can't be overstated how important reviews are to help a book reach the people it's intended to help. If you have taken something positive from reading this book, please spare five minutes of your time to help someone else find their something positive too. You never know where it might take them.

Even just a rating and one sentence will make a big difference.

2. Tell someone about this book

Do you know someone who always talks about the book they'll write or the business they'll start or the creative project they've just thought of? Maybe they never start. Or maybe the habits, relationships and mindsets they have don't enable their best work.

Please Share Your Work: Free E-book

If you want to make a difference, you have to start and you have to keep going. You have to do what it takes to create the conditions to do your best work.

And if you want to make a difference, at some point your work has to connect to someone else. I want your work to make a difference and that's why I'm giving you a draft copy of the fourth book in the 12-Minute Method series *for free*.

To get your copy visit

www.robbieswale.com/12minute-method-downloads

or scan this QR code:

This book, provisionally titled *How to Share Your Work Even When You're Scared*, contains more practical inspiration aimed at getting your idea out into the world.

The full book will be published in late 2022, but this draft version will always be free to you via the above link.

Stay Up to Date About The 12-Minute Method

This is the third in a series of books, created to support you through the creative process. The final book in the series will be published later in 2022.

To be the first to hear about that book, other 12-Minute Method developments, and my other work, sign up to my mailing list at:

www.robbieswale.com/mailing-list

Acknowledgements

Written on 19th July, 2022

I'm still not quite sure whether writing my acknowledgements with a 12-minute timer is a good thing or not.

But, here goes.

First of all, thank you to you – you read this book and you are here reading the acknowledgments. That means a lot to me.

I almost always read the acknowledgements of books. I do this because it matters to me to understand who the important people are, whom the book wouldn't have existed without, in whose absence it would have been a different book.

That feels especially important in this book, a book about creating the conditions for great work.

There are so many people who have helped me create the conditions for this book to emerge.

First are the multitude of influences on what I have written here. More than in any other book in the series, this is a work of collecting ideas that have made a difference to me. I have learned these from books, friends, training courses, coaching clients and more. I am deeply grateful to everyone whose name I have mentioned in this book and those whose ideas have influenced me but didn't get mentioned. Without all of you, my work wouldn't be as good and this book wouldn't be as good. I owe you all one. Let me know when I can pay you back.

Second, the people who have practically worked on this book.

Steve Creek, for the conversation in Doppio Coffee in Battersea which catalysed what these books became, and for editing this book to help make my writing better and the book more impactful.

Tim Pettingale and Joseph Alexander helped form this series into what it is and gave me the 12-Minute Method name.

Stefan and his team at Spiffing Covers did great work on this cover and the covers in the rest of the series.

Friends, colleagues and fellow adventurers like Alex Swallow, Michael Hubbard and particularly Joni Zwart have test-read bits of the series at different points, giving important feedback – and if there's anyone else who's done this who I've forgotten, at least I have the 12-minute excuse. Joni also gave me great feedback on what I might do with the series and what mattered as I took it out into the world. Thank you.

When I think of the people who have really helped me create the conditions for great work, my coaches and mentors have contributed as much as almost anyone in helping me transform towards the person I am today. Mike Toller, Rich Litvin, Katie Harvey, Robert Holden: thank you.

My oldest friends, members of a WhatsApp group of many, many names, have made me laugh and stopped me feeling alone. Laughter is as great a catalyst for great work as isolation is a cause of people giving up.

My family taught me curiosity, love and how to create the conditions for great conversation – all of these make me so grateful to have come from that place and to still have those people.

Reading this book back as part of my final run at the manuscript, I was genuinely caught off-guard by how much it moved me. One of the places where tears came into my eyes was the chapter, Love is a Transformational Practice. It really is.

Emma and Leah, you have transformed me and continue to transform me. You help me be proud to be me, give my life meaning when it feels meaningless and have loved me so much that it has become almost easy to love myself.

Lastly, thank you to everyone who has appreciated and encouraged me in these last seven years and before. Every email, conversation, LinkedIn message or comment, book review and more. They have all made a difference.

Intellectually I often find it hard to absorb them, but each of them is a part of who I am now, and so each of them is a part of the work that I do, helping me start new things, keep going, and keep creating the conditions for greatness.

Thank you.

How I Wrote a Book in 12 Minutes: A Few Notes About the Process

For those who are interested, I wanted to add a few words about how this book was created, and the idea of creating a book in 12 minutes, to supplement what I described in the introduction and throughout the book. I share this to give those among you who want to do something similar the power to choose how you do that.

I originally imagined that this series would simply be a compilation of the pieces as they were posted online, but once something starts to become a book (or a series of books), some extra decisions need to be made.

First, it felt important to give myself a little more leeway than I do with the articles when they first go online. I gave myself an extra proofread of the whole book and then sent it to my friend, Steve Creek, a professional copy editor, to give it a once-over.

The spirit of those edits was to improve it, so it could support people even more. It was to tighten and clarify. The substance of the articles was not changed significantly – a sentence was added or removed here and there, a few titles made more relevant or punchier. There were a few tweaks to make the language and sense clearer, or to fix bits that were hazy on detail because the original was written in 12 minutes and there wasn't time to look up precisely what someone had said. After the book came back from Steve, there was some broader feedback and some rearranging of the pieces. Then it sat, pretty much untouched, for about two years (more on that another time).

When I came back to it, with the help of self-publishing entrepreneurs Tim Pettingale and Joseph Alexander, we realised it would work even better as a series. That required another edit from me, again leaving the substance but tightening and making clearer a sentence here and there, or adding a few words or a couple of sentences to make it clear why a particular piece belonged here, in this part of the book or series.

As the publishing process went on, the book received another edit from Steve and another two reads and light edits from me. I noticed, as each time passed, that I was more willing to tweak for clarity and impact, and to more firmly place a piece where it sat in the book. But, as you can tell from reading, these pieces are absolutely imperfect, and many are pretty much the same as when they were originally written on the train or with the 12-minute timer.

At different stages, I also added introductions to each part, to help tie the book together. Those introductions, the notes and pages about free gifts, and this piece are the only bits not originally written in 12 minutes, although even with the introductions (which mostly didn't take 12 minutes) I set the timer to make sure I got out of my own way and got going. That's how I work. The 12-Minute Method section at the start was written in the same spirit, but I had to reset the timer four times to have time to say everything that needed saying (The 48-Minute Method!).

A few pieces from the series of articles didn't quite belong in a series about creating what you are called to create, so those were removed. Remarkably few pieces from the first three years of the writing practice overlapped in content enough that a piece needed to be removed, but there were a couple, so they came out. I felt that a few more didn't help the flow of the books, so they came out too. This process was surprisingly hard, but it served the books to remove them. All these pieces can be read on LinkedIn where they were originally posted, on my website, or in a short eBook called *The Cutting Room*, available at:

www.robbieswale.com/12minute-method-downloads

I wasn't sure where to draw the line with which set of 12-minute articles would make up the series, but on my deadline to send the book to Steve I realised it was three years and one day since I started the weekly practice (after the initial five pieces). So, what makes up this book and the other three in the series are the five original parts of The Train Series and almost exactly three years of weekly articles.

And that, pretty much, is how you write a book (or four!) in 12 minutes.

Printed in Great Britain
by Amazon

18696581R00119